TARGETED TRAINING

TARGETED TRAINING

A "How To" Guide for

Changing Employee Behavior

in 30 Minute Intervals

Dennis O'Connor/Penny Drain

To order additional copies of this book, contact:
Xlibris Corporation
1-888-795-4274
www.Xlibris.com
Orders@Xlibris.com
64421

Table Of Contents

Why It's Time To Change

*The biggest threat to your business is employees who
don't demonstrate the right behaviors!*

*By the time your traditional employee training program gears up to
address the problem, you will have lost customers
and potentially be out of business!*

I T'S NO SECRET that hard times place enormous stresses on
businesses and governments. However, a more sinister threat has
been eating away at the private and public sectors for the more than 30
years—regardless of economic conditions.

This threat metastasizes each time an employee fails to do the "right"
thing, disregards a customer's needs or fails to follow standard operating
procedures. The result is poor quality, dissatisfied customers, a co-worker
lawsuit and/or reduced sales.

The worst part of this scenario is that those behaviors are enabled by
YOU!

You the executive leadership team, *you* the line supervisor, *you* the
training professional and *you* the uncomplaining employee who struggles
to stay focused during yet another three-day training session, while a pile
of work sits waiting for *you.*

In desperation, *you* will commit to more training, where a larger set of
facts will be jammed into a smaller window of time. And at the end of the last
training day, as you stagger out of the stale air of an over-crowded training
room, perhaps it will dawn on you . . . **it's not just what employees know,
it's *how they behave* that will save or strangle your enterprise.**

We passionately believe the future of any company lies in the heads,
hearts and hands of its workers.

Effective training is more than just transferring information. There's
simply too much of it out there. Unless it cuts through the clutter and

personally grabs us, we tend to tune out and shut down. We are aware of the critical need to move workers to want to *use and apply* the information that is at their fingertips, so that training is worth your investment.

Last year, and for countless years before it, private businesses and governmental units have invested hundreds of thousands of dollars in employee training programs.

And for good reason . . . Our nation's education system is not designed to prepare anyone for the specific behaviors needed to be successful in the workplace. Traditional educators do a slightly better job with "skills" training, but only in a generalized manner, often failing to connect those skills with on-the-job performance.

When global economic conditions turn downward, it only furthers these challenges as many "trained" employees are asked to pitch in and perform unfamiliar duties. Likewise, other "displaced" workers find themselves forced to confront completely new workplace settings where day-to-day expectations do not correlate to prior experience.

How do companies solve these problems?

On the pages that follow, you will find sufficient detail to answer that question. But before we begin, let's shed some out-dated mindsets—concepts and ideas that have been sucking energy out of our organizations; misconceptions like:

1. Commitment to employee training is best measured by the number enrolled and how many days they are in class
2. Curriculum shouldn't mix soft skills with hard facts
3. More material equals better business results
4. "Take Away Binders" ensures knowledge retention
5. Learning is best accomplished in a classroom setting
6. Positive feedback about a class equals effective training
7. Technology makes training cheaper and more effective

These relics of conventional thinking are the sirens that lure companies into sending their employees to countless training seminars. And, when "outside" training proves too expensive, these businesses turn inward and ask their internal training departments to copy the same 1-day, 3-day or week-long training format.

Regardless of whether the session is internal or external, the message to employees is we want you to *"take" training*; like take a break or take a leave of absence.

Thus, enrolled employees disappear from their jobs for substantial periods of time, which results in a loss of productivity and an extra expense for the company. Likewise, we inadvertently separate the knowledge gained from the work to be done . . . within minutes of returning to work, those fancy training binders begin collecting dust as workers scramble to catch up with tasks that have piled up for them.

Meanwhile, the organization's management relaxes; secure in the knowledge that they have made a significant investment in training. They have done all they can to promote increased job performance, right?

Wrong!

Sequestering *adult* learners in a "traditional" classroom setting for up to 8 hours a day isn't the way to improve performance; it's a way to demoralize your employees. Think about what occurs during those eight hours. Employees are:

- Lectured like children—a bombardment of facts
- Buried by tons of content to read—an information "dump"
- Focused on deficiencies—job skills finger-pointing

In spite of these conditions, some employees:

- Return to work highly motivated, but only if the content was personally interesting—and only if it was delivered by an energetic facilitator
- Retain some level of motivation for up to six weeks
- Remember a few of the main concepts

Such outcomes can hardly be considered a solid return on the investment (ROI). This traditional approach falls short because:

- Too much information is delivered during long, 8-hour days
- There is no transfer of learning from the classroom to workplace

Recent research on the human brain confirms that people process information better in shorter chunks. Yet, companies remain stubbornly convinced that the best "bang for the buck" comes from jamming as much material as possible into the shortest space of time.

That mistake won't be made here. *This book is purposely short.* You will get the facts you need in the fewest words possible. And, key points will be repeated to help foster retention.

If you were looking for a doorstop, this guidebook will likely disappoint you (*other training tomes might better fit that bill*).

Now, two short chunks to get you started:

1. *"How" you train your employees is more important than "what" you train them!*
2. *Shortening the amount of time between learning and applying dramatically increases results—just-in-time training!*

INTRODUCTION

HOW—not WHAT

I T'S VERY ADMIRABLE for both the private and public sectors to invest money and resources into training. However, when economic times are tough, many business entities are quick to cut training budgets, even though they know they are making a long-term mistake.

But, for the sake of our discussion, let's not focus on WHAT should be done. After all, most successful businesses understand the value of a highly trained and motivated workforce. Rather, let's examine HOW employees get their training:

- How do adults learn?
- How do we change behaviors in the workplace?
- How do we open up lines of communication among employees and various departments in an organization?
- How do we reinforce the concepts learned?
- How do we give employees "Just-In-Time" training to address current business needs?
- How do we "proactively" develop *behaviors* as well as job skills?

That's the focus of this book.

It's Time to Revolutionize Your Training!
It's Time to Change the System!

. . . and the solution is waiting for you.

It's called TARGETED TRAINING!

- TARGETED TRAINING is FOCUSED.
- TARGETED TRAINING is HARD CORE.
- TARGETED TRAINING is FLEXIBLE.

TARGETED TRAINING is supervisor-led courseware, packaged in multiple *Single Topic Lessons*, designed to quickly—and effectively—focus on a specific business issue or problem that requires real-time impact. Ideas that must be taught IMMEDIATELY to your employees to ensure that the wrong behaviors are stopped and the right things start happening today.

TARGETED TRAINING enables companies to offer employees the better of two critical learning components:

- Just-in-Time (as needed) educational experiences
- Personalized, supervisor-led interventions

This book takes you step-by-step through the "basics" of setting up your own TARGETED TRAINING system. We'll explain to you the "Business Rationale" for why it works, and we'll explore the many "benefits" of this revolutionary instructional tool.

We'll also explain, in depth, the various components of each TARGETED TRAINING "module." We'll show you how to conduct Pilots, mini-Train-the-Trainer sessions and a detailed Launch Meeting that will help you implement and cascade the TARGETED TRAINING process throughout your organization.

We also will discuss the importance of a Matrix Analysis and the value of an Audit, which ensures that your TARGETED TRAINING program is getting maximum results for your organization.

You may choose to leverage the concepts in this book to inspire your training department to move in a new direction. Give a few copies of this book to the opinion leaders in your training group and start working toward your training revolution. This approach often works well in mid-sized companies where the influence of a few individuals can be felt throughout the organization.

However, for the larger organizations, you may want to ensure that this approach doesn't get buried underneath all the other good ideas your training department is trying to handle. In that case, it may be wise to give us a call (248.880.5000) so we can help you operationalize the process.

TARGETED TRAINING is a very strong (*and culturally sensitive*) initiative that will positively transform your organization, when executed properly.

Just ask UAW-Ford!

SPECIAL THANKS TO UAW-FORD

B EFORE WE BEGIN, we must tell you the UAW-Ford story. It all began in 2003, thanks to a great visionary—Dan Brooks. Brooks, representing the UAW, was Co-Chairperson of the Quality Department for all 60+ Ford manufacturing facilities nationwide. "Quality" wasn't a household term at that time until Brooks implemented a system-wide standardization process, highlighted by TARGETED TRAINING.

When Brooks began to revise Appendix Q in the 2003 Collective Bargaining Agreement, he had a vision to train his members more effectively. He clearly understood that UAW members and Ford supervisors badly needed training to learn and reinforce Quality processes at their local facilities. He also knew that training takes a lot of time, which conflicts with production and scheduling demands at local facilities.

So, how do you combine both objectives—with a FOCUS ON QUALITY?

> *"Our vision was to deliver just-in-time training in simple modules that focused on important Quality issues," Brooks explains. "We all know there is need to learn new concepts, refresh our skills and properly communicate among our work groups on various Quality issues—but we needed to accomplish this quickly, so we're not wasting valuable time at our locations."*

Brooks' vision, called TARGETED TRAINING, became a reality when he hired us to create and develop more than 115 modules and 26 different Quality courses, launched to all North American plants and facilities served by Powertrain, Vehicle Operations, Visteon and Ford Customer Service Division (FCSD).

> *"The response was tremendous," Brooks said of the launch. "Local facilities were energized because TARGETED TRAINING focused specifically on Quality issues. We piloted all the courses, and the feedback was overwhelmingly positive. People wanted us to focus on Quality—and TARGETED TRAINING was the answer to their educational needs."*

It was a challenge for Brooks to get this training project approved.

"During these tough, cost-containment, economic times, there is more and more pressure to keep employees on the production line," said Brooks. "There's minimal time for training, especially a 4-hour or 1-day course. Yet, we always need to examine Quality processes, and give employees information so they can apply that knowledge to their jobs. TARGETED TRAINING was the perfect solution."

The results? In only four years, Ford Motor Company took that long, hard climb to the top of *J.D. Power* Quality Rankings—ahead of Toyota. **Now, Ford sets the Quality standard in the automotive industry.**

"That's the beauty of TARGETED TRAINING," Brooks explains. "Every course is TARGETED to specific skills levels and employee needs. We want training to be a meaningful experience. We want people to learn Quality concepts quickly—and then apply them to their jobs. That's how we focus everyone on the importance of Quality."

Two years later, Brooks, now one of UAW's top Leaders, asked us to create similar TARGETED TRAINING curricula for his Equality & Diversity and Health & Safety (OSHA) departments. We've had a great partnership for many, many years. It's also been very beneficial to all the hard-working members at UAW-Ford.

Thanks, Dan.

Onward & Upward!

—Dennis (DOC) O'Connor
and Penny Drain

## CHAPTER 1

What Is "Targeted Training?" (Overview)

TARGETED TRAINING IS another in a series of Continuous Improvement initiatives that help standardize operations in many production-based industries, including manufacturing, health care and public-sector entities.

Over the years, it has become a *Best Practice* for many instructional initiatives.

Why?

Because many organizations are beginning to learn that it's time to stop *dumping* large amounts of information on your employees, once a year, and then checking off "Training" from your list of things to do.

Your employees need to *buy into training* as an ongoing process, not a one-time event. More importantly, your employees need to KNOW what they should be doing on the job—at all times.

The concept of TARGETED TRAINING recognizes that training (*regardless of the subject matter*) should be FOCUSED on the behaviors of individual employees. Whether it's a Quality issue, a Safety concept, a Customer Service process, a Diversity policy or simple "basic skills" refresher courses, employees need to *learn and apply* concepts that FOCUS on doing their jobs in a smarter and more effective way.

That's what TARGETED TRAINING is all about!

The original TARGETED TRAINING program was launched by the UAW-Ford National Program Center's Quality Department in 2005, as part of the contractual enhancements in Appendix Q of the 2003 Collective Bargaining Agreement.

TARGETED TRAINING focuses on specific business issues. It strives to open the lines of communication between employees and managers in a "Just-in-Time" basis—so you can *proactively* address concerns quickly and effectively.

TARGETED TRAINING is not a "flavor of the month" concept.

- TARGETED TRAINING is FOCUSED.
- TARGETED TRAINING is HARD CORE.
- TARGETED TRAINING is FLEXIBLE.

TARGETED TRAINING really works!
TARGETED TRAINING is:

- Valuable information delivered in 30-minute segments
- Focused on one concept
- Delivered by supervisors or managers, who are trained
- to be effective facilitators
- Highly measurable with Pre-Tests and Post-Tests included in each module
- Conducted in a meeting room so employees and work groups can interact on a specific subject
- Highly interactive—and flexible
- Easily accessible. TARGETED TRAINING modules are printed and launched from your own computer network

The instructional process is as follows:

- ♣ 5 minutes—Administer Pre-Test
- ♣ 5 minutes—Employees read the Single Topic Lesson
- ♣ 10 minutes—Leader conveys Single Topic Lesson
- ♣ 5 minutes—Conduct Discussion/Questions & Answers
- ♣ 5 minutes—Administer Post-Test
  30 minutes

Please Note: *The process could last as long as 45 minutes to 1 hour, depending on the amount of time available and the issues/concepts being discussed.*

TARGETED TRAINING is not dependent on sophisticated computer technologies:

- Single Topic Lessons (STLs) are created in a Microsoft-Based applications (i.e. Word, Publisher, Excel, PowerPoint)
- STLs are transformed into PDF files for content control purposes (You don't want ad-hoc changes to the training content)
- Each PDF file then is placed on your computer network or web intranet site for easy access within your organization

DENNIS O'CONNOR/PENNY DRAIN

TARGETED TRAINING *nomenclature*

For the purpose of this discussion, we define TARGETED TRAINING "lessons" as *Modules.* There are three components to each TARGETED TRAINING "module":

o Single Topic Lesson. (Print as many as you need from the PDF file, based on the number of employees attending the course)
o Facilitator Guide.
o Test. Each module features Pre-Tests and Post-Tests (the same test), so that we can measure the learning, based on information employees received from the Single Topic Lessons

All TARGETED TRAINING "modules" are facilitator-led. The modules are designed so supervisors and/or work group leaders (*acting as facilitators*) can deliver a concept in a memorable, 10-minute "Single Topic Lesson" format.

Multiple TARGETED TRAINING modules are created so organizations have a *comprehensive curriculum* on specific subjects or processes.

Single Topic Lesson

A Single Topic Lesson is a short and concise educational tool on a particular subject intended for quick delivery and focused-information sharing.

Single Topic Lessons are delivered in **10 minutes**.

The entire "learning intervention" is as follows:

o Within a Single Topic Lesson, "Key Elements" are included down the left column
o Detailed learning concepts are in the right-hand section
o Each Single Topic Lesson focuses on understanding specific LEARNING OUTCOMES—behaviors that are expected and applicable to the job

Facilitator Guide

A Facilitator Guide is a tool for the supervisor to use to prepare for the session. It includes 5 common sections:

1. **Before the Lesson**—*Facilitator Preparation*
2. **"BEST" Presentation Tips**
3. **During the Lesson**—*Aiding Facilitators on delivering Single Topic Lesson content*
4. **Ask Discussion Questions**—Focused on "localizing" the concept with specific questions about your local area
5. **Summary/Post-Test**

Test

The Test is a measurement tool to establish an employee's current knowledge level or to verify learning after a lesson. The Test usually is "informational/objective" in nature (*True/False, Multiple Choice and/or Fill-in-the-Blank questions*).

The same test serves as the pre-test and post-test.

- *Pre-Tests* are administered before the lesson to help determine an employee's current knowledge level. The Pre-Test is administered to the appropriate employees or work group before (in advance of) the scheduled training course.
- *Post-Tests* are administered after the lesson. The Post-Test is intended to ensure knowledge transfer. Once all employees have had adequate time to complete the post-test, it is reviewed as a group. Employees are allowed to retain their copy of the post-test during this review.

Additional details of each component of a TARGETED TRAINING module are further reviewed and discussed in Chapter 4.

Curriculum Analysis

TARGETED TRAINING modules can be developed from existing curriculum, or it can be developed "from scratch" if curriculum doesn't exist.

For example, the "foundation" of one company's TARGETED TRAINING Diversity curriculum came from a highly-acclaimed 8-Unit training series, which was launched nationally in a series of 1-day seminars to all their employees in the early 2000's.

Since that time, many employees have retired, while others have been newly hired. It would have been very costly to re-launch this live, 1-day seminar to all the new employees.

Yet, the Diversity information was critical and needed to be delivered. Likewise, the company told us that several current employees had forgotten (*or didn't demonstrate the knowledge of*) many Diversity concepts that were taught almost nine years in the past. A reinforcement strategy did not exist for this training initiative.

So, we took that 1-day course and developed 33 TARGETED TRAINING modules for the Diversity Department. In this curriculum, 29 modules came from the existing materials, and we created four new modules to address new and specific business issues, as they pertained to discrimination and harassment concerns. We packaged the modules and called them *Tools for Success*. This company now has a *complete library* of training modules that can be used at any time to address specific Diversity situations.

In addition to this curriculum, we also provided two separate, 2-hour Orientation Training programs (*4 Targeted Training modules—30 minutes each*)—all designed in a TARGETED TRAINING format for easy delivery and maximum learning.

The first of the two Orientation programs was focused on NEW EMPLOYEES. We took the highlights of the 1-day Diversity seminar and condensed them into a 2-hour program for all NEW EMPLOYEES. The Orientation also included a newly-created "Policy Module," so NEW EMPLOYEES can review all the company's Diversity-related policies and procedures **BEFORE** they begin employment.

The second of the two Orientation programs was focused on NEW APPOINTEES. This 2-hour program was very similar, in content, to the New Employee Orientation program . . . however, the focus of this training was on employees who were placed into new positions, perhaps Leadership or work group leader roles.

The NEW APPOINTEE may have never needed to interact with other employees on a group or team basis. The NEW APPOINTEE also may need additional job skills and training on how to properly communicate with fellow workers in a "team" or "leadership" role. This Orientation helped those employees learn some basic skills, in terms of handling various Diversity issues and situations.

Curriculum Path

We organized the Diversity Targeted Training modules in a *Curriculum Path*. (*A sample curriculum path may be found in the Appendix D, which contains numerous TARGETED TRAINING examples.*)

This curriculum path was divided into three distinct areas of instruction.

What?—These are basic, foundational, knowledge-based modules, focused on various Diversity concepts. These TARGETED TRAINING modules are for individuals who are new to the company, or for existing employees who need a refresher or reinforcement of the 1-day Diversity Seminar.

- New employees should learn these modules AFTER receiving the Diversity Training Orientation Program
- These WHAT modules should be reviewed and taken as a prerequisite to the HOW modules

How?—The "HOW" modules are the skill and application-based courses. These modules are for individuals who are not demonstrating and/or applying the lessons learned in the WHAT knowledge-based modules.

Why?—These modules answer the question: *"Why is Diversity considered a priority?"* These modules are for individuals who do not understand or demonstrate the importance of a specific business issue within the company.

In addition to these three sections, we added a category for "Geographic and Operating Unit" Topics. These topics featured *newly-created* modules to address additional Diversity business needs.

This category on the Curriculum Path addressed current situations and helped managers and employees "proactively" resolve concerns that may occur on a day-to-day basis.

This newly-created section was a great way to *update* existing training materials and make them more relevant to today's Diversity issues.

A Revolutionary Instructional Tool

TARGETED TRAINING is considered by many educational experts as a *Revolutionary Instructional Tool* that will be used by many organizations in the future.

Some professionals have "branded" TARGETED TRAINING as the "30-30" Instructional System. This is an easy way to explain the benefits of TARGETED TRAINING within your .

Over the years, we are very aware of the various "branded" television news-magazine programs:

- 60 Minutes
- Dateline
- 48 Hours
- The Situation Room
- 20-20

The easiest way to explain TARGETED TRAINING is to talk about this new and exciting way to learn by using the "*30-30*" method of teaching:

- One lesson every *30 days* (monthly)
- Each lesson is *30 minutes* long
- No more day-long or week-long seminars
- No more long lectures filled with too much information
- Training is *focused* on learning one concept at a time
- Reinforcement of that concept or specific behavior is accomplished on a "Just-In-Time" basis
- Modules should be taught at least on a monthly basis for maximum effectiveness
- However, the "flexibility" of TARGETED TRAINING allows organizations to deliver a module *immediately*, when a business problem needs to be addressed

## CHAPTER 2

Benefits of Targeted Training (Business Rationale)

Business Case

TARGETED TRAINING IS *"Change You Can Believe In,"* to quote our 44th President.

Times HAVE changed! Businesses no longer can afford to have employees "away on training" for days and weeks at a time.

Think about it. Gone are the days when companies had extra employees on the floor to "cover" for someone who was enrolled in a training class. Today, and for the foreseeable future, there will continue to be more and more pressure to keep employees at their workstation, on the floor or on the production line.

Scheduling is critical.

There's no time for training, especially 4-hour or 1-day courses. Yet, we all know there's a need to learn new concepts, refresh our skills, collaborate with other employee groups, re-examine processes, focus on quality, remember safety rules, learn new technologies, understand diversity, etc.

And employees need this information *immediately*, so they can apply the knowledge to their jobs right away.

There is still a huge demand and need for training workshops, especially when they are focused on changing behavior rather than lecturing to employees.

But rarely is there TIME to take a day-long course because of the demands on our business.

Perfect *"Just-In-Time"* Solution

One approach touted over the past two decades has been computer-based training.

This application works in some cases. It's a "Just-in-Time" (*as needed*) experience, but there are many drawbacks:

- It's impersonal—the computer can't answer all your questions about a subject. You need the help of a live facilitator
- It's highly dependent on a strong IT infrastructure
- It's highly dependent on updated computer technologies, which sometimes are a costly budget item
- Not all work stations have enough computer equipment to implement web-based training
- It's remote—and very isolated. You lose the ability to "interact" with other employees, which is an important part of the learning experience
- You also lose the ability for supervisors and employees to have a conversation about a specific business issue

TARGETED TRAINING is a "Just-in-Time" experience that solves the downside issues of computer-based training.

- Modules are created in a Microsoft-Based application (i.e. Word, Publisher, Excel, and PowerPoint)
- Modules are transformed into PDFs files for security purposes. We don't want employees changing the training content
- Each PDF file then is placed on your own computer network for easy access within your organizations

Benefits

TARGETED TRAINING isn't a dream.

This "cutting-edge" learning application has received outstanding accolades from Fortune 500 companies, along with other smaller production-based companies.

- The Single Topic Lessons (STLs) are very concise
- The STLs are very informative
- Employees like the "quick-and-easy" format to learn information

- The STLs also are being used as New Employee Orientation applications—to quickly introduce new people to new concepts
- The STLs have helped promote more "communication" and involvement within work groups
- The STLs are flexible. You aren't hindering production schedules.
- Employees receive the 30 minutes of training when it "fits" everyone's schedule—during a weekly meeting, on the hospital floor, at your workplace, on a plant production line, when production is slow, when a line is down for maintenance . . . or when there's a critical need to learn a new concept or address an immediate problem

Easy to Facilitate

Supervisors and/or work group leaders are helped by the TARGETED TRAINING (TT) format. The TT modules are workable "chunks" of training information that help "facilitators" deliver the training to their employees. The TT modules are designed to engage the employees through an interactive process, complete with tests, multi-media interaction and discussion questions.

Let's be honest.

Are your employees really going to learn everything they need to know on the job if 4 days of information is *dumped* on them once a year?

The 30-minute "chunks" are based upon the average attention span of an employee, and his or her ability to retain course knowledge. If a group of individuals come to training . . . and they have different job grades, skill levels, or just plain learn at a different pace . . . the system can simultaneously provide different courses, or different levels of the same course, to each individual.

Why Rely on Supervisors to Deliver Training?

- The "quick answer" is BUDGET and FLEXIBILITY. Clearly, it's more cost-effective for your supervisors to deliver TARGETED TRAINING on a "Just-In-Time" basis.
- But the "hard answer" is the need to DEVELOP your supervisors into good coaches and to ask them to act as a "support system" to your

employees when they need help on the job. Employees will better remember concepts when they are taught by people (managers) they see every day on the job—people whom they know and whom they have developed a relationship with over the months and years.

That's the beauty of Targeted Training!

Targeted Training offers you the "flexibility" to deliver multiple modules any time during the day, week or month—especially when supervisors observe a poor behavior that needs to be monitored and corrected IMMEDIATELY. That's the best way for employees to apply and learn concepts focused on specific job functions.

Another benefit of having your leaders deliver

TARGETED TRAINING is that it *forces conversation* between supervisors and employees on specific business issues that aren't normally discussed during the work day. Our experience shows that this "conversation" is very beneficial because it helps to monitor and evaluate an employee's behavior and overall performance.

Likewise, it also forces supervisors to learn new concepts on-the-job, so they aren't embarrassed when they talk to their employees.

Reinforcement Tool

Our experience is that most organizations are quick to launch training programs, but they forget to develop a Reinforcement and Comprehension Strategy. Both hourly and salaried workers return to their work and are EXCITED about what they learned. That excitement lasts about six weeks to two months. Then, learning comprehension begins to evaporate, negatively affecting a company's results.

Suffice to say, **millions of dollars** are spent on training programs annually—with no idea as to if, how and to what extent, training is impacting business results.

That's not the case with TARGETED TRAINING. In fact, many companies use TARGETED TRAINING as a "reinforcement tool" for their existing curriculum.

Research indicates people need ongoing communication to reinforce (*and comprehend*) the knowledge and skills learned at various training programs. Communications must focus on:

- APPLYING consistently what was learned in the training initiatives
- REINFORCING the training objectives
- COMPREHENDING the training content
- DEVELOPING Active learning (fun and interactive), instead of Passive learning (lecture-based)—to SUSTAIN THE EXCITEMENT!"

That's what TARGETED TRAINING is all about!

Transfer of Learning

The quick "Single Topic Lesson" approach allows work teams to get trained during scheduled and unscheduled downtime. It also allows your work teams to focus on process discussions and possibly identify process improvements.

TARGETED TRAINING may be enhanced with various "observation tools," such as performance checklists. This way, employees can prove a *transfer the learning* from what was discussed in the classroom to how they apply those concepts on the job. Supervisors may "sign off" on the tool when they see the employee demonstrating the behavior.

(A sample Observation Checklist may be found in the Appendix D, which contains numerous TARGETED TRAINING examples.)

As a *Revolutionary Instructional Tool,* the TARGETED TRAINING approach will lead to increased individual and team performance, as well as better products and service delivery . . . making it a win-win for all!

Positive Feedback

All TARGETED TRAINING modules should be "Piloted" *before* they are deemed final and placed on your computer network in PDF format. (*See Chapter 6 for more information on the Pilot process.*)

As we refined the TARGETED TRAINING method, dozens of Pilots were conducted on everything from the right amount of knowledge to convey to the best training cadence to use.

We learned a lot from our Pilots. (*Details are discussed in Appendix A.*) *Here are some of the highlights:*

- 96% of the employees registered improved test scores from their pre—to post-tests—TARGETED TRAINING WORKS!
- Focusing content on a single topic area increases retention and understanding—Single Topic Lessons (STLs)
- 95% of training content receives positive ratings—when presented as STLs
- Managers can effective deliver STLs after a minimal amount of preparation (a 30-minute Train-the-Trainer)
- Most importantly, everyone liked the idea that lessons focused on a single, specific business issue—across the board "buy-in" for training

Other comments and observations we capture:

- The Single Topic Lessons are very concise
- The Single Topic Lessons are very informative
- Employees liked the "quick-and-easy" way to learn usable information
- The Single Topic Lessons were seen as helping to promote more communication and involvement within work groups
- The Single Topic Lessons were considered powerful *communication tools*, as well as *training tools*, which helped managers address current "hot button" issues in the workplace
- The Single Topic Lessons are easy to follow
  We believe this comment speaks to the layout of our STL handouts which is based on Visual Learning concepts, such as the appropriate use of colors and managing the flow of information across the page

- The Single Topic Lessons helped people learn more

  We interpret this as comment about knowledge retention, which is consistent with adult learning study that shows adults have a hard time remembering numerous concepts taught in day-long or week-long courses

- TARGETED TRAINING and Single Topic Lessons are very flexible

  These comments mostly came from managers and internal training personnel. In probing deeper, we have come to believe the perception of flexibility is based on the ability to fit STLs into normal production schedules. Employees are receiving 15-30 minutes of training when it "fits" everyone's schedule—during a weekly meeting, at their workstations, when production is slow, when the system is down for maintenance, or when there's a critical need to address an immediate issue

DENNIS O'CONNOR/PENNY DRAIN

## CHAPTER 3

The Matrix Analysis

THE DEVELOPMENT PROCESS for TARGETED TRAINING is very powerful:

1. Single Topic Lessons (STLs) are developed from **existing training courses** thus leveraging prior investments; or STLs can be freshly minted to address emerging business issues
2. STLs are based on agreed-upon "Learning Outcomes" that ensure *behavioral change* in the workplace.
3. STLs also are based on agreed-upon *SKILL LEVELS* of each employee's job classification
4. The modules then are crafted and *focused* to align with the specific courses, specific learning outcomes and specific skills levels of each employee.

That's what makes it TARGETED!

The Matrix Analysis

The days of "learning new information" in a traditional classroom setting should have ended years ago. Businesses and governmental entities don't have time (*or the budget*) to send employees off to simply "learn new information."

In today's marketplace, leading businesses demand a rapid *transfer of learning* from the classroom to the workplace. These businesses want to see *behavior change* come out of the classroom. It's one thing to teach a concept or skill. But it's imperative that adult learners APPLY THAT SKILL when they return to their jobs.

Put another way, the "foundation" for the design and development of each TARGETED TRAINING module is based on establishing the correct *Learning Outcomes* for each module.

This is in direct conflict with the "traditional" approach of identifying specific *Learning Objectives* for each training activity. Learning Objectives are not critical to TARGETED TRAINING because our focus is on *behaviors* and a *transfer of learning* for every concept taught in a Single Topic Lesson.

Therefore, the up-front needs analysis must focus on identifying and developing specific *Learning Outcomes*, based on each specific skill levels and job descriptions or classifications of your employees.

Defining Learning Outcomes

Employees need to *learn and apply* concepts that FOCUS on doing their jobs in a smarter and more effective way.

Learning Outcomes are defined as what employees NEED TO KNOW on the job. In other words, what is *essential* for employees to properly perform their job function? During the process of developing Learning Outcomes, it's important to differentiate between what is a "Need to Know" job function vs. what is a "Nice to Know" job function.

Because of this, it is not uncommon to develop a "Matrix" of Learning Outcomes for employees who have BASIC, AVERAGE and/or ADVANCED skill levels within an organization.

The "Matrix Analysis Process

"The Matrix Analysis" process includes the following steps:

1. Meet with program Subject Matter Experts (SMEs) to validate and/ or identify specific *Learning Outcomes* for each existing course or for each newly-created course
2. Validate these *Learning Outcomes* based on specific job descriptions and/or job classifications
3. Research/Develop/Write the *Learning Outcomes* for each course
4. Gain SME Approval of all the *Learning Outcomes*
5. Gain Department Approval of all the *Learning Outcomes*

After completing the up-front analysis, it is best to document these understandings in a "The Matrix Analysis." The Matrix Analysis serves as the foundation for the development of all Single Topic Lessons within the TARGETED TRAINING curriculum.

CHAPTER 4

The Components

THE FOLLOWING IS an explanation (*with specific samples*) of the components of a TARGETED TRAINING module. As discussed earlier, the instructional process is as follows:

- ♣ 5 minutes—Administer Pre-Test
- ♣ 5 minutes—Employees Read the Single Topic Lesson
- ♣ 10 minutes—Leader Conveys the Single Topic Lesson
- ♣ 5 minutes—Conduct Discussion/Questions & Answers
- ♣ 5 minutes—Administer Post-Test
   30 minutes

Please Note: The process could last as long as 45 minutes to 1 hour, depending on the amount of time available and the issues/concepts being discussed

Single Topic Lesson

A Single Topic Lesson (STL) is a short and concise educational tool on a particular subject intended for quick delivery and focused information sharing. Single Topic Lessons are delivered in 10 minutes.

The entire "learning intervention" is as follows:

- Within a Single Topic Lesson, "Key Elements" are included down the left column
- Detailed learning topics are in the right-hand section
- Each STL focuses on teaching specific Learning Outcomes—*behaviors* that are expected and applicable to job operations

---

SAMPLE
RESPECTFUL COMMUNICATION
TARGETED TRAINING
Single Topic Lesson

Showing Respect

There are significant differences in the ways people of different nationalities, cultures, races and genders communicate. As part of getting to know one another, **it will help a lot if we take the time to discover what is respectful** -- and what is disrespectful -- to a person of a different sex, race or nationality.

☐ One of the things you will discover is that people often <u>signal disrespect</u> without meaning to — and without being aware of it.

☐ A second thing is, perhaps, more important: You need to find ways to show respect, and avoid the accidental insult.

By doing this, you will find out how those you may have always thought are different, strange or inferior are, in fact, very much like yourself — not at all strange, and definitely an equal.

"Showing Respect" means honoring every person, and respecting their individual dignity as human beings. While it is true that people of different cultures and upbringings use somewhat different ways to signal respect, there are a few "universal" ways to show respect to another person.

1. Attentive and **active listening.** Everyone all over the world, regardless of different cultures and habits, love to be listened to.

2. Deliberately finding ways to **praise and recognize** other people for what they do, what they have done, or simply what they are. Complimenting another person is a way of saying, "I care about you," which, in turn, is a powerful way to communicate respect.

3. **Maintaining your self-control,** whenever there is a conflict or difference of opinion, particularly if (and when) another person verbally attacks you. This is not easy to do, but it's possible if you remember a few simple rules:

   ☐ DON'T ignore insulting behavior or language.
   ☐ DON'T just run away and hide when others attack you.
   ☐ DON'T just "take it" when you are insulted or hurt.
   ☐ DON'T become angry and aggressive.

   ☐ DO "count to 10" and take a deep breath before you respond.
   ☐ DO use a calm, steady, non-emotional but firm tone of voice and posture.
   ☐ DO tell the individual how his or her behavior makes you *feel*, and/or how it *impacts* you -- using "I-statements," such as *"I am upset when you use that kind of language."*
   ☐ DO keep listening, especially when the other person is excited. Don't give in, but do try to understand. Eventually, this removes the emotionality from the situation.
   ☐ DO try to work out a solution to problems that is satisfactory to both of you. Remember, "win/win" is the objective; "win/lose" or "lose/lose" results in frustration, disappointment and often a desire for revenge.

Facilitator Guide

A Facilitator Guide is a tool for the supervisor to use to prepare for the session.

It includes 5 common sections:

1. **Before the Lesson**—*Facilitator Preparation*

   - Review the Single Topic Lesson
   - Review the Facilitator Guide
   - Gather local processes
   - Review the "purpose" of the lesson

2. **"BEST" Presentation Tips**

   - Incorporate the following bullet tips as cornerstones of good presentations:

     - Be Prepared!
     - Enthusiastic delivery, Emphasize key Topics, Encourage questions.
     - Speak clearly, loudly, and confidently.
     - Tell participants what you're going to tell them (state purpose), then tell them (deliver lesson), then tell them what you told them (summarize).

3. **During the Lesson**—*Aiding Facilitators on delivering Single Topic Lesson content*

   - Conduct, correct and collect the pre-test tool
   - Distribute the Single Topic Lesson
   - If feasible, review the pre-tests as participants read the Single Topic Lesson
   - During instruction, read aloud each section in the Single Topic Lesson where the test answers can be found. This helps to emphasize key elements missed in the pre-test
   - Engage participants and review the information

4. **Ask Discussion Questions**—Focused on "localizing" the concept with specific questions about your local area

5. **Summary/Test**

   - Restate the purpose of the Single Topic Lesson to summarize

- Advise participants that use of the Single Topic Lesson is allowed while taking the post-test
- Distribute the post-test to participants and give them 5 minutes to complete **INDIVIDUALLY**
- After completing the post-test, review **AS A GROUP** to ensure transfer of learning

Sample Facilitator Guide

 **SAMPLE**
RESPECTFUL COMMUNICATION
TARGETED TRAINING
Facilitator Guide

Before the Lesson:
- Review the Single Topic Lesson (STL).
- Review this Facilitator Guide.
- Understand that the purpose of this Single Topic Lesson is to use respectful communication when handling diversity-based communication and conflict issues.
- Use examples of respectful and disrespectful communication occurring in your facility to help illustrate the concepts in this lesson.

BEST - Presentation Tips:

Incorporate the following bullet points as cornerstones of good presentations:

- Be Prepared!
- Enthusiastic delivery, Emphasize key points, Encourage questions
- Speak clearly, loudly, and confidently
- Tell participants what you're going to tell them (state purpose), then tell them (deliver lesson), then tell them what you told them (summarize).

During the Lesson:
1. Introduce the STL by reviewing with participants the purpose stated in the *Before the Lesson* section -- why participants need to know this and what participants need to do with it.
2. Distribute the Pre-Test tool and allow participants time to complete (approximately 5 minutes).
3. Explain that the purpose of the test is to determine participants' knowledge of the lesson.
4. Collect the Pre-Test tool and then distribute the STL and allow a few minutes for participants to read. As participants read the STL, review the Pre-Test and make sure you emphasize points that the participants missed.
5. Use STL to discuss how respectful communication can impact diversity-based communication and conflict issues.
6. Review the information in the left-hand column by stressing the following points:
   - Differences in ways that people of different nationalities, cultures, races and genders communicate
   - Need to discover what is respectful and disrespectful
   - Similarities in how people of different nationalities, cultures, races and genders communicate
   - Lead a discussion of the differences and similarities based on various nationalities, cultures, races and genders *(see suggested discussion questions below)*
7. Explain what showing respect means.
8. Emphasize the "universal" ways to show respect:
   - Attentive and active listening
   - Deliberately finding ways to praise and recognize other people
   - Maintaining self-control (including Dos and Don'ts)

Ask Discussion Questions:
- Based on your nationality, culture, race, and/or gender, how do you communicate?
- What does showing respect mean to you?
- What is the impact of the Dos and Don'ts of maintaining self control?

Summary and Post-Test:
- Restate the purpose of the Single Topic Lesson to summarize.
- Distribute the Post-Test to each participant and give them 5 minutes to complete **INDIVIDUALLY.**
- After completing the Post-Test, review **AS A GROUP** to insure transfer of learning.

DENNIS O'CONNOR/PENNY DRAIN

Test

A Test is a measurement tool to establish an employee's current knowledge level or to verify learning after a lesson.

The Test usually is "informational/objective" in nature (*True/False, Multiple Choice and/or Fill-in-the-Blank questions*). The same test serves as the pre-test and post-test.

Pre-Tests are administered before the lesson to help determine an employee's current knowledge level. The Pre-Test is administered to the appropriate employee or work group before or in advance of the scheduled training course.

Pre-Test Process

- Explain that the purpose of the pre-test is to determine participants' knowledge of the lesson
- Distribute the pre-test tool. Read each test question aloud, allowing time for the participants to answer the questions (Approximately 5 minutes total)
- Collect the pre-test tool and then distribute the Single Topic Lesson (STLs) and allow a few minutes for participants to review. If feasible, review the pre-tests as participants read the STL
- During instruction, read aloud each section in the STL where the test answers can be found. This helps to emphasize key elements missed in the pre-test

Post-Tests are administered after the lesson.

The Post-Test is intended to ensure knowledge transfer. Once all employees have had adequate time to complete the test, the test is reviewed as a group. Employees are allowed to retain their copy of the post-test during this review. Employees' questions are clarified and employees are coached, as required, with appropriate follow-up on any test questions they did not understand or did not correctly answer.

Post-Test Process

- Advise participants that use of the Single Topic Lesson is allowed while taking the post-test
- Distribute the post-test to participants and give them 5 minutes to complete **INDIVIDUALLY**
- Once all employees have had adequate time to complete the test, the test is reviewed as a group
- Employees are allowed to retain their copy of the post-test during this review
- Employees' questions are clarified, and employees are coached as required

Sample Test

> ### _SAMPLE_
> ### RESPECTFUL
> ### COMMUNICATIONS
> _TARGETED TRAINING_
> Test
>
> 1. Showing respect means:
>
>   A. Honoring every person.
>   B. Honoring those who respect me.
>   C. Respecting the individual dignity as human beings.
>   D. All of the above
>   E. A and C
>
> 2. Strategies for showing respect include:
>
>   A. Attentive and active listening
>   B. Praise and recognition
>   C. Maintaining self-control
>   D. All of the above
>
> 3. Place a check mark next to what you should DO when maintaining your self control:
>
>   __ Ignore insulting behavior or language
>
>   __ Run away and hide when others attack you
>
>   __ "Take it" when you are insulted or hurt
>
>   __ Become angry and aggressive
>
>   __ "Count to 10" and take a deep breath before you respond
>
>   __ Use a calm, steady, non-emotional but firm tone of voice and posture
>
>   __ Tell the individual how his or her behavior makes you _feel_, and/or how it _impacts_ you -- using "I-statements," such as "I am upset when you use that kind of language"
>
>   __ Keep listening, especially when the other person is excited. Don't give in, but do try to understand. Eventually, this removes the emotionality from the situation.
>
>   __ Try to work out a solution to problems that is satisfactory to both of you. Remember, "win/win" is the objective; "win/lose" or "lose/lose" results in frustration, disappointment and often a desire for revenge.

DENNIS O'CONNOR/PENNY DRAIN

The TARGETED TRAINING Process

In addition to the actual delivery of a Single Topic Lesson, the TARGETED TRAINING process should feature:

a. Preparation
b. Localization of Issues
c. Pre-Test
d. Discussion/Dialogue
e. Interaction/Active conversation on local issues
f. Multiple Post-Tests
g. Multiple On-the-Job Observations
h. Follow-up
i. Reinforcement/Transfer of Learning of the training message

## CHAPTER 5

The Developmental Process

"Having the vision is no solution . . . Everything depends upon execution."

TARGETED TRAINING IS guided by a customer-focused, quality-oriented, creative approach which pays attention to detail, *behavioral learning* and creativity.

The following is a "Checklist" for Writing Targeted Training Modules:

Overall

√ Use the Matrix Analysis document to focus on learning outcomes *(behaviors that are expected and applicable to job operations)*
√ Determine topics that will address the learning outcomes
√ List those topics in a Curriculum Path document

Tests

√ Use learning outcomes to write pre/post tests for each Single Topic Lesson (STL)
√ The test usually is "informational/objective" in nature (*True/False, Multiple Choice and/or Fill-in-the-Blank questions*)

Single Topic Lessons

√ Write each Single Topic Lesson (STL) based on the learning outcomes and pre/post tests
√ Focus each STL on one concept, idea, behavior, etc.

√ Keep the STL focused on what the participants "need to know" versus what is "nice to know"

√ Include an explanation of "key elements" versus "details" of the topic

√ Use appropriate graphics in the Single Topic Lesson

Facilitator Guide

√ The Facilitator Guide is divided into 5 common sections:

- ♣ Before the Lesson
- ♣ "BEST" Presentation Tips
- ♣ During the Lesson
- ♣ Ask Discussion Questions
- ♣ Summary / Tests

√ When you write the **Before the Lesson** section, provide preparation directions regarding:

- ♣ The materials that should be reviewed
- ♣ The local samples (examples) etc. that should be considered presented during the lesson
- ♣ Clarifying the purpose and the learning outcomes of the STL
- ♣ Include "BEST" Presentation Tips—Incorporate the following bullet tips as cornerstones of good presentations:

  - ♣ Be Prepared!
  - ♣ Enthusiastic delivery, Emphasize key Topics, Encourage questions
  - ♣ Speak clearly, loudly, and confidently
  - ♣ Tell participants what you're going to tell them
  - ♣ (state purpose), then tell them (deliver lesson), then tell them what you told them (summarize)

√ When you write the **During the Lesson** section, provide directions for:

- ♣ Conducting, correcting and collecting the pre-test tool
- ♣ Distributing the Single Topic Lesson
- ♣ Reviewing the pre-tests as participants read the Single Topic Lesson
- ♣ Reading aloud each section in the Single Topic Lesson where the test answers can be found. This helps to emphasize key elements missed in the pre-test
- ♣ Engaging participants and reviewing the information

√ When you write the **Ask Discussion Questions** section focus on "localizing" the Single Topic Lesson with specific questions about their facility, area, department, work station, etc.

√ When you write the **Summary/Test** section provide directions for:

- ♣ Restating the purpose of the Single Topic Lesson
- ♣ Advising participants that use of the Single Topic Lesson is allowed while taking the post-test
- ♣ Distributing the post-test to participants and giving them 5 minutes to complete INDIVIDUALLY
- ♣ Completing the post-test and reviewing it AS A GROUP to ensure transfer of learning

DENNIS O'CONNOR/PENNY DRAIN

## CHAPTER 6

Conducting Pilots and
Train-the-Trainers

O NCE YOUR TARGETED TRAINING modules have been drafted, all the Single Topic Lessons within the curriculum should be thoroughly piloted *before* rolling them out to all the employees in your organization.

The purpose of the Pilots is to "test" the design and content of the TARGETED TRAINING materials to ensure the modules are meaningful and *actionable* to your employees.

The "hidden" benefit of piloting TARGETED TRAINING has been the energy and enthusiasm generated from the "pilot employees".

To date, companies using the TARGET TRAINING approach have experienced phenomenal results from their Pilot sessions.

In general, these organizations found that only minor content adjustments were required and that the piloting process actually *created a marketing pull* for the training material. In many cases, upon completion of the Pilots, those organizations immediately received requests from the field for copies of the training materials.

The Pilot Process

Obviously, it is critical that TARGETEDTRAINING be user-friendly, functional and measurable.

To accomplish this, it is important that you get participation from supervisors and work group leaders in your Pilot. These are the individuals who will *coach and advise* employees at each location on how to use TARGETED TRAINING materials. The goal is to develop these supervisors and leaders into advocates who can also lead TARGETED TRAINING sessions.

You should plan to spend one full day with the "facilitators" (*selected supervisors and/or work group leaders*) in a detailed Train-the-Trainer session—prior to executing the Pilot sessions.

At this Train-the-Trainer class, you should:

o   Review the TARGETED TRAINING materials
o   Focus on the Facilitator Guide as the primary "tool" for delivery
o   Explain/demonstrate the pre—and post-test process
o   Review/prepare for specific courses each facilitator will teach in the pilot sessions
o   Conduct "live" practice sessions in front of peers—with complete observation
o   After the session, offer one-on-one coaching, if needed and requested

After the Train-the-Trainer session, the balance of the Pilot (*multiple days if multiple modules need to be piloted*) should feature the newly-trained "facilitators" delivering multiple Single Topic Lessons (STLs)—one after the other.

o   The "students" in the Pilot should be a mix of people from different departments in your organization
o   Each classroom should contain no more than 10-15 students for maximum effectiveness

To help conduct a Pilot session evaluation, we advise organizations to use three (3) different measurement scales:

1) *Session Evaluation*—to help measure the effectiveness of the Single Topic Lessons
2) *Facilitator Observation*—to help measure the effectiveness of the Facilitators and the Facilitator Guides
3) *Test Analysis*—collecting, grading and evaluating all individual pre-tests and post-tests to help measure the effectiveness of each quiz question:

   a. Were the questions easy to understand?
   b. Were the questions tied to the Learning Outcomes?

c. Were the questions—and answers—tied to the Single Topic Lessons?

d. Was there improvement (*transfer of learning*) from the pre-tests to post-tests?

(*A sample of the Evaluation Tool and the Observation Tool may be found in the Appendix D, which contains numerous TARGETED TRAINING examples.*)

Enhanced Pilot Format

Some organizations have extended Pilot sessions *beyond the classroom* to ensure a more "real-world" application to TARGETED TRAINING. They have successfully piloted selected training courses in an actual area near the employees' workplaces.

For example, in some manufacturing or medical organizations, the pressure to *stay on the production line* or *complete the floor shift* makes it nearly impossible to conduct training in a meeting-room setting.

This is another area where the TARGET TRAINING approach excels. Because of its just-in-time format TARGETED TRAINING can be accomplished on the plant floor or at a designated hospital station.

When a 30-minute window presents itself, managers can simply pull the TT module down from their network, print materials from a local printer, and hand out the information. Within minutes, that manager can deliver the Single Topic Lesson and begin the process of changing workplace behaviors.

CHAPTER 7

The Launch

F OLLOWING THE PILOT, you are ready to LAUNCH the TARGETED TRAINING materials to your employees.

- Content corrections from the Pilot should be made to all TARGETED TRAINING modules *prior to Launch*
- The corrected modules (electronic files) then should be converted to PDFs and posted on your company's computer network *prior to Launch*

As with all program launches, we recommend that local "Training Coordinators" and/or "Training Champions" attend a centralized meeting to review the TARGETED TRAINING materials, and to acquaint themselves with the "implementation process." Adding this short meeting (typically 4-6 hours) to your roll-out plan ensures consistency in how TARGETED TRAINING reaches every employee at every level of your organization.

At this meeting, you should present your newly developed (*and piloted*) TARGETED TRAINING curriculum.

You should:

- Reinforce the VALUE of TARGETED TRAINING, and discuss how to use the modules on a day-to-day basis
- Review all the modules in your curriculum
- Review the Curriculum Path
- Review how to access each module from your computer network
- Review the TARGETED TRAINING process, and focus on "How to Deliver" Single Topic Lessons

Suggested Launch Meeting Content

1. Overview Your TARGETED TRAINING Program

    o   Scope of the Project
    o   Philosophy of TARGETED TRAINING
    o   Why you created these specific modules
    o   Deadlines for Delivery/Implementation at your local facilities

2. Share Pilot Results and Feedback
3. Present your Curriculum Path and discuss how to use it
4. Review Sample Modules

    o   Single Topic Lessons
    o   Facilitator Guides
    o   Tests

5. Discuss "Applying the Training"—Delivering a specific module around a specific Business Need
6. Focus on How Adults Learn in Different Ways

    o   How to Deliver Single Topic Lessons
    o   How to "Engage" the Audience
    o   Presentation Tips

7. Present how to use "Discussion Questions" for maximum effectiveness
8. Review the Test Process and Philosophy
9. Show how to navigate your computer network or web intranet site to obtain various TARGETED TRAINING modules
10. Review the Cascading Process—so that every manager, supervisor and employee "touches" TARGETED TRAINING

Cascading at each Local Facility

Phase I: *Developing an Implementation Plan*

- Review all TARGETED TRAINING materials and Curriculum Path to develop your local training implementation plan
- Review the appropriate training needs based on The Matrix Analysis and job classification/group listing
- Identify what curriculum component, at which level, is required for a given employee or work group
- *Recommendation:* Directors and/or Top-level Managers should be involved in this planning process

Phase II: *Preparing Leadership for Implementing TARGETED TRAINING*

- Access the required materials
- Review any supplemental materials
- The supervisor and work group leader should review the Facilitator Guides for each Targeted Training module
- Location Training "Champions" and/or Training "Coordinators" should share each Single Topic Lesson (STL) with the location's top managers
- All top directors and managers should review the TARGETED TRAINING materials with their supervisors and work group leaders prior to presentation to an employee or work group. This ensures that all concepts become embedded knowledge throughout the organization
- All top managers must ensure that their supervisor and work group leader are adequately familiar with the material, *know the content* and are capable of delivering the Single Topic Lessons effectively
- Supervisors and work group leaders need to *present and deliver content* effectively. Sample Delivery Tools should be reviewed with supervisors prior to conducting a TARGETED TRAINING session.

CHAPTER 8

The Evaluation Process

A UDITS ARE CRITICAL to organizations because what ***gets audited gets done***. Just as external auditing teams are used to ensure that high standards are met, it is equally important to audit the implementation, delivery and results (*transfer of learning*) of your TARGETED TRAINING initiative.

Audits should be conducted at various "random" facilities to ensure that local locations demonstrate an understanding of the importance of cascading and delivering TARGETED TRAINING—and to reinforce that TARGETED TRAINING is here to stay.

To work best, audits should be conducted by personnel NOT in your local organization. If possible, to maintain independence and objectivity, auditors should be training professionals who are external to the company.

External auditors should make their first visit to your facilities about 3-6 months *after* your TARGETED TRAINING launch.

After one year, the same auditors should re-visit those facilities that need extra help in the implementation and/or delivery process on an *as-needed basis.*

Purpose of the Audit

The purpose for a TARGETED TRAINING audit is to ensure:

- Proper implementation of your TARGETED TRAINING curriculum
- Standardized implementation of TARGETED TRAINING
- A transfer of learning is occurring at each location

If possible, auditors should visit both "high performing" and "low performing" facilities in your organization.

- High performing locations—To benchmark the "Best of the Best" and to share those results with other locations
- Low performing locations—This group represents the majority of the audits, so that auditors can make the appropriate corrections on-site

Audit Process

An external Auditor (Assessor) spends one (1) full day at each facility to:

o Assess the TARGETED TRAINING effectiveness

   (A sample of an Audit "Checklist" may be found in the Appendix D, which contains various TARGETED TRAINING examples.)

o Meet with various internal top managers to introduce the evaluation process and to review their implementation plan
o Observe a few TARGETED TRAINING sessions to determine how supervisors and/or work group leaders are delivering the training
o Interview a random sample of supervisors and/or work group leaders and employees regarding the transfer of learning
o Meet with top managers, again, at the end of the day to debrief and develop Action Plans in preparation for the next visit

The Assessor then documents the findings:

o Develops a detailed, comprehensive, written report for the assessed facility and for your overall organization
o This report should include the results of the evaluation with details about on how effectively TARGETED TRAINING is being applied at the workplace. Evaluations of effectiveness are based on whether:

- The facility implemented TARGETED TRAINING based on the standardized implementation process
- Proper implementation of the TARGETED TRAINING curriculum is being demonstrated
- A transfer of learning is occurring at each location

## CHAPTER 9

Creating A "Culture" For Targeted Training

NOW THAT WE'VE taken you through the entire "How To" steps for executing a TARGETED TRAINING initiative . . . How will you really know whether or not your organization is "ready" to embrace the TARGETED TRAINING approach?

Simply put, how can an organization "create a culture" for TARGETED TRAINING?

There are many variables involved, but some of the underlying conditions are more obvious:

1. Is there a *budget commitment* for "traditional" training?
2. Is there a *time commitment* for "traditional" training?
3. Do your employees meet or exceed the *behavioral expectations* of their specific job function?

If the answer is "NO" to any of these three questions, then your organization would benefit from instituting a TARGETED TRAINING approach.

Some variables are not so obvious.

Business Need

The business need for TARGETED TRAINING is clear if not quite obvious:

- To establish a reinforcement and follow-up strategy for existing training
- To involve members and employees in discussion and interaction

- To ensure retention of training materials
- To observe and document on-the-job application and a transfer of learning AFTER the training is delivered

In addition, to job skills curriculum, we have noticed organizations building a business case for using a TARGETED TRAINING approach for:

- Roles & Responsibilities courses
- New-Hire Orientation courses
- New-Hire Appointees (*refresher courses for transferred employees who are assigned new positions with Leadership/Managerial responsibilities*)

Mission

The mission is equally straight forward:

- To create a culture where there is a *relentless daily focus* on specific business issues (i.e. Quality processes, Health and Safety procedures, Customer Service initiatives, Diversity and Discrimination policies, etc.)
- To ensure that people have the necessary training and tools to perform their jobs effectively
- To ensure application and transfer of learning relative to all training concepts
- To create a "continuous thinking environment"

  o Where employees are constantly talking about, and asking questions about, specific business issues related to the training
  o Where managers and leaders are quick to *proactively* respond to these issues when they arise

Culture Problem

In many organizations, employees participate in "traditional" training sessions:

- Viewing videos,
- reading handbooks,

- attending long seminars,
- reading information posted on the board,
- reading policy letters,
- exploring information on the web site,
- reviewing various processes

There is:

- Minimal Discussion
- Minimal Interaction
- Minimal Dialogue
- Minimal On-the-Job Observation
- Minimal Follow-up
- Minimal Reinforcement/Sustainment of the training message

In some cases, there is *no proof* that any "learning" takes place:

- Do employees understand it?
- Do they retain the information?
- Do they know how to apply it?
- Do they have a transfer of learning?

Culture Solution

Developing and delivering a focused TARGETED TRAINING curriculum—so a *library* of TARGETED TRAINING modules *(Single Point Lessons, Facilitator Guides and Tests)* is available on an as-need basis to train employees BEFORE a problem occurs.

1. The lessons, alone, don't work. Traditional training seminars are quickly forgotten.
2. Supervisors and/or work group leaders must embrace and use the Facilitator Guides in the Targeted Training modules to ensure behavioral-based learning.
3. Targeted Training modules must contain pre-tests, post-tests and observation checklists, so you can properly measure a "transfer of learning" from the classroom to the workplace.

That is the POWER of TARGETED TRAINING—measuring a transfer of learning.

Roles & Responsibilities

The *cultural change* process should start with everyone understanding his/her *Individual Roles & Responsibilities*, as they pertain to specific business issues.

(A sample Roles & Responsibilities Single Topic Lesson may be found in the Appendix D, which contains numerous TARGETED TRAINING examples.)

Announcement (Rollout) Meeting

As your TARGETED TRAINING curriculum is being developed, it would be beneficial to conduct a "rollout" or announcement meeting with the same local "Training Coordinators" and/or "Training Champions" assigned to launch your TARGETED TRAINING initiative (see Chapter 6).

At this meeting, you should present and teach the "Individual Roles & Responsibilities" Targeted Training Module—complete with Action Plans and an enhanced Facilitator/Conversation Guide for "1-on-1" On-the-Job Observations.

This module serves as the *foundation* for executing future Targeted Training modules:

- This module begins to *create a culture* where there is a relentless daily focus on the specific business issue
- This module helps ensure that people have the necessary training to do their jobs
- This module begins to ensure the "transfer of learning" and the application of key information included in the training materials
- This module opens the lines of communication, so employees will feel comfortable to ask questions about various business issues
- This module helps Leadership respond quickly to problems as they arise

After the Announcement Meeting, the "Champions" should go back to their facilities and cascade these *1-on-1 conversations* on overall Roles &

DENNIS O'CONNOR/PENNY DRAIN

Responsibilities to every level of your organization—starting at the very top managerial levels at each location.

These conversations should take place BEFORE the Targeted Training curriculum is launched, so that supervisors will discover *immediately* from their members and employees what "training issues" need to be addressed. This will also allow employees to give *instant feedback* to you, so you can quickly incorporate the information into the development of future TARGETED TRAINING modules.

Follow-up—As part of a "continuous thinking environment," supervisors and/or work group leaders should consistently conduct 1-on-1's after the launch of the TARGETED TRAINING curriculum, so that additional training or issues will be discovered and addressed immediately.

If you follow these steps, you are well on your way to creating a positive *culture* for TARGETED TRAINING.

APPENDIX A

Positive Feedback

TARGETED TRAINING ISN'T just a wild, unproven concept.

- It's been piloted
- It's been implemented
- It's been audited
- And it's been audited, again, by an independent company

TARGETED TRAINING really works!

The response has been tremendous!

For example, plant employees for one of major company have become highly energized because TARGETED TRAINING modules focused specifically on their unique, local business needs.

We gathered the following feedback from Leaders/Managers, Supervisors, Work Group Leaders and Employees:

- The TARGETED TRAINING modules are flexible. You aren't hindering production schedules
- The curriculum is available on an "as-needed" (Just-In-Time) basis for EVERYONE
- Employees receive the 15-30 minutes of training when it "fits" everyone's schedule—during a weekly meeting, when a production line is down for maintenance, or when there's a CRITICAL NEED to learn a new concept or address an immediate problem
- This is a proactive strategy to training, rather than a reactive action when a problem surfaces on the plant floor or at a workplace

The following pages contain some additional "highlights" from various feedback reports:

Pilot Reports

The purpose of the Pilots is to "test" the design and content of the TARGETED TRAINING materials—*before launch* to the local plant facilities (*see Chapter 6 for details*).

Key Findings

The Pilots were outstanding—in the classroom and at the plant site. In terms of evaluating training content, we successfully met (*or exceeded*) our various measurement criteria.

1) *Session Evaluations*—Very positive results. Most employees graded the training with 4's and 5's—on a scale of 1-5; 1 being the WORST and 5 being the BEST. More than 95% of the participants liked the Single Topic Lessons format.

   a. Quick
   b. Easy to read
   c. Graphically pleasing
   d. Good information, presented in a concise manner

2) *Observations*—Facilitator Guides worked, as designed. The facilitators (*supervisors and work group leaders*) understood the process most of the time—the value of a pre-test and post-test, how to deliver the lesson, how to connect the lessons to the participants' jobs and how to "personalize" the information to their local facility.

   a. We had *limited time* to prepare the supervisors and/or work group leaders to deliver the training, but they still understand the process. So, the Facilitator Guides worked.
   b. Learning was limited only when facilitators did not follow the Facilitator Guide.

3) *Tests*—Test analysis revealed that a "*transfer of learning*" stayed the same or increased from the pre-test to the post-test—*more than 96%* of the time.

Overall Pilot Themes/Conclusions

1) The Single Topic Lessons were "on target."

   a. Curriculum is sound. Content is good.
   b. Materials are easy to understand.
   c. 30-minute training format is genuinely received as a *passionately positive* way to conduct training in the future.
   d. Single Topic Lessons are considered very *flexible*—and have multiple uses:

      i. New Employee Orientation
      ii. Reference materials
      iii. Refresher courses
      iv. Communication tools
      v. Work Group meeting tools

2) Facilitator Guides are the "key" tool to ensure that Learning Outcomes are met, and that there is a true transfer of knowledge.

   a. If supervisors follow the Facilitator Guides, as designed, then the training will be very successful.
   b. If facilitators choose not to follow the Facilitator's Guide, then the training won't be as effective.
   c. It is imperative that facilitators (*supervisors and/or work group leaders*) follow the Facilitator Guides to ensure a proper transfer of learning. If they try to *wing it*, then the training won't be as successful.

3) Tests (pre and post) were very powerful—and welcome—tools for learning. No one objected to the testing—at all.

4) If possible, use of color and graphics elements are recommended on all TARGETED TRAINING modules—for ease of learning.

Feedback indicated that TARGETED TRAINING works:

- The Single Topic Lessons are very concise
- The STLs are very informative

- Employees like the "quick-and-easy" format to learn information
- The STLs also are being used as a component of New Employee Orientation—to quickly introduce new people to the organization
- The STLs have helped promote more "communication" and involvement within work groups
- The STLs are considered to be powerful *communication tools*, as well as *training tools*, to help address current issues in the workplace
- The STLs are easy to follow
- The STLs promote retention. Adults have a hard time remembering numerous concepts taught in day-long or week-long courses
- The STLs are graphically pleasing. Visual learning (with use of multiple colors) enhances the educational experience
- The STLs are flexible—you aren't hindering production schedules. Employees receive 15-30 minutes of training when it "fits" everyone's schedule.

Do People Learn?

After piloting a 33-module TARGETED TRAINING curriculum on Diversity, we learned the following:

- Qualitatively, based on the discussions that we witnessed (and the "positive and immediate" behavior change in both groups), it was clear that a lot of learning took place.

  - Participants were eager to discuss issues
  - Participants were excited about learning the next modules

- Quantitatively, from the Pre-Tests and Post-Tests, more questions were answered correctly on the Post-Tests—on ALL but one of 33 Modules.

  - Concepts were learned after each STL
  - Concepts were clarified after each STL
  - There was a transfer of learning

- The Pre-Tests and Post-Tests were INVALUABLE in charting whether or not people learned the concepts taught
- The "Discussion Questions" were the highlight of each module. It was more than "reviewing" a Single Topic Lesson. Participants were given the opportunity to discuss issues and, in some cases, resolve open issues.

Audit Reports Reveal Measurable Results

After launching a 115-module TARGETED TRAINING curriculum for a Quality Department in the manufacturing sector, we learned, through a detailed auditing procedure, that TARGETED TRAINING made a significant difference at many facilities—and behaviors changed.

As we conducted each audit, we focused on one important principle:

TARGETED TRAINING should result in a transfer of learning demonstrated by behavioral changes

Overall, we found that a *transfer of learning* was occurring at most facilities. TARGETED TRAINING was being *applied* at the workplace.

- There was *Better Awareness* of Quality issues
- We saw behavioral changes, as it pertains to Quality
- Employees started to ask questions after each TARGETED TRAINING session
- They began to think of better ways to accomplish a task, in terms of Quality improvement
- We observed that Quality issues began to surface and many were being resolved quickly

Results/Findings

- Plants told us they appreciate the *"flexibility"* of the TARGETED TRAINING curriculum
- Many plants followed our suggested "Curriculum Path" to roll out the TARGETED TRAINING courses

- Plants also told us (and we observed) that TARGETED TRAINING was very well received by younger employees. They appreciated the focus on Quality, and sought more information.
- Many plants showed a stronger commitment to Quality, and TARGETED TRAINING:

  - Leadership was involved in the cascade process—starting at the very top of the organization
  - Facilitators "engaged" employees to participate in all the training sessions
  - Facilitators prepared BEFORE delivering each module. They used "local examples" to help explain Quality concepts written in the TARGETED TRAINING modules.
  - Plants "tailored" the Curriculum Path to meet their local business needs and to address immediate Quality problems
  - Plant Managers and Quality Engineers incorporated TARGETED TRAINING discussions into daily "work-arounds" or morning "set-up" meetings.

- When some plants just "went through the motions" to comply with the TARGETED TRAINING initiative, we discovered the following concerns:

  - Leadership was NOT involved in the cascade process
  - Area Managers and Superintendents rarely saw a Single Topic Lesson, and did not take the time to support supervisors during the delivery process
  - Facilitators "read" the Single Topic Lessons (STLs) to employees with minimal discussion
  - Facilitators did not prepare BEFORE delivering a module. They did not use "local examples." They were more worried about making sure everyone signed the attendance sheet.
  - Plants used the Curriculum Path, but did not bother to examine/analyze what courses might be most important for their employees to learn immediately
  - There was no designated "champion" to keep the momentum going during the implementation process

Best Practices

- The most successful TARGETED TRAINING sessions we observed occurred when facilitators took the time to find local examples of the subject being taught
- Some plants are wisely using "downtime" as a way to implement TARGETED TRAINING. It is part of their regular routine.
- Some plants are taking the Single Topic Lessons off the web site and re-formatting them into PowerPoint presentations—one concept is placed on each slide for better retention
- When Single Topic Lessons are properly cascaded throughout the plants, we found that the high-performing plants *involved* top management personnel in the process
- Many plants utilized "Sponsors" in the room when supervisors and/or work group leaders delivered TARGETED TRAINING modules—to help answer questions

Impact on Results

We found that TARGETED TRAINING is making a difference in many of the local facilities—and creating a positive impact on Quality. For example:

1) ***Plant #1***—Where employees reported that "numbers" are *decreasing* on "high rates of missing things." One specific department is catching mistakes now, versus before TARGETED TRAINING. They are more aware of Quality issues, and the numbers reflect that.
2) ***Plant #2***—Leadership went above-and-beyond the minimum test requirements. They collected EVERY pre-test and post-test to quantifiably prove "transfer of knowledge." In one class that was observed, the aggregate pre-test score on *Control & Reaction Plans* was 67%. After the lesson, the post-test score was 95%.
3) ***Plant #3***—Employees gained tremendous awareness of Error Rate Reports (*during the Error Rate TARGETED TRAINING module*), so they began to ask many questions about the various reports. Shortly thereafter, officials saw that metrics w*ent down from 2.0 % to 1.5%*

against objective on a specific error-rate report—because *employees now understood the* value and importance of minimizing errors.

4) While not quantifiable, there is qualitative evidence that TARGETED TRAINING greatly increased *awareness* of Quality issues throughout all the plants we observed. Employees and operators began to ask questions after each TARGETED TRAINING session. They then began to think of better ways to accomplish a task, in terms of Quality improvement.

Audit Conclusions

- Feedback remained very positive
- There is an increased "focus" on Quality issues
- TARGETED TRAINING is an effective tool to help employees embrace the "challenge of change"
- Most employees have incorporated TARGETED TRAINING into their daily routines
- TARGETED TRAINING has made a "positive impact" on Quality

Independent Audit Report

In addition to our internal audit of TARGETED TRAINING, one of our clients felt the need to conduct an "independent" assessment of the project to further verify the success of the learning activity. The following is an excerpt from that report:

Effectiveness: A measure of the degree to which TARGETED TRAINING achieved its strategic purpose and program-level goals.

Purpose and Goals:

The major goals for TARGETED TRAINING defined both by its stated learning objectives and by senior leadership, were the following:

- Increase awareness of Quality
- Transfer knowledge of Quality best practices to all levels on the factory floor

- Provide a focused, targeted approach to train people at the appropriate level
- Inaugurate a structured workforce knowledge *assessment process*
- Increase skill levels in order to improve quality as envisioned by the company's Quality Operating System.

Strengths:

Against those goals, TARGETED TRAINING succeeded in several important respects:

- It was highly effective in raising awareness among the entire workforce and others about Quality and the various methods for dealing with Quality issues
- It was effective in transferring knowledge about Quality and Quality improvement
- A large majority of workers trained under TARGETED TRAINING are still applying knowledge learned
- It had a positive impact on product Quality
- Target dates for full implementation of the training were met

Quality: A measure of the Quality of TARGETED TRAINING's implementation planning, curriculum and training delivery

Planning and Curriculum—Strengths:

Interviewees at all levels were strongly positive about the "quality" of the curriculum:

- TARGETED TRAINING created a well-respected "quality curriculum," based on Single Topic Lessons, that is comprehensive, targeted to different levels and adaptable to individual plant needs
- It demonstrated the value of STLs as a means of delivering training in a short period of time on specific Quality issues
- It included a methodology for assessing pre—and post-training impacts on individual knowledge levels
- It created a "common nomenclature" for Quality

Feedback Summary

Supervisors, work group leaders and operators all were very excited about these training materials.

- They were very enthusiastic about this training project
- They liked the format
- They liked the focus on a specific business issue
- Employees liked how the Single Topic Lessons (STLs) served as communication tools with their Supervisors, as well as strong training materials
- Course content was rarely changed *(about 95% of the courses received positive ratings by all the Pilot groups)*. Evaluation forms were completed at the end of the day for every Pilot session.
- Most complemented the "ease of the process"—simple, quick, easy to understand, not time consuming
- Most complemented the "look/design" of the lessons. They liked the various "graphic" treatments.
- Most liked how the materials all linked to a specific business issue and a specific Learning Outcome
- Most did not object to the testing process. In fact, they enjoyed it—because it challenged them to demonstrate what they learned in the classroom or meeting room.
- Employees felt that they learned a lot from the interaction and group discussions by sharing actual examples and experiences from their operations/facilities
- The Facilitator Guides were useful and supportive
- The Pilot sessions were good because the participants are able to provide feedback, assessments of material, and needed corrections/clarifications in material before launching the program
- Utilizing supervisors/work group leaders to present the material was a "plus" for the initiative
- The Single Topic Lessons promoted interaction within the group
- The Facilitator's Guide provided discussion questions to help drive group participation
- The Supplemental Materials and other Train-the-Trainer materials used to prepare the supervisors were critical to the program's success.

They should be highly recommended and included in the launch/implementation process.

- The Single Topic Lessons were very concise; quick and easy-to-learn information
- They liked the "flexibility" of each module—that you can customize and personalize each lesson for individual, local locations
- Everyone complemented the "ease of the process"—simple, quick, easy to understand, not time consuming
- Everyone liked the testing process

  o No one was "threatened" by the quizzes
  o Everyone understood the pre-and post-test goals—it WAS NOT an individual test that counted against them
  o Everyone liked that the questions were reviewed "as a group" at the end of the training

    - They really wanted to know if they got the answers correct
    - They wanted to know if they learned something
    - We witnessed "transfer of learning"

- Many employees said they would use the lessons as "good reference" materials
- Participants also liked that they weren't given stacks and stacks of paper to read. They liked the one-page format of the Single Topic Lesson.

Testimonials

Dan Brooks,
UAW Assistant Director
National Programs Center

"The response to TARGETED TRAINING has been tremendous. It has become an important component to our successful Standardization process. Local facilities are energized because TARGETED TRAINING focuses specifically on Quality issues. We piloted all the courses, and the feedback was overwhelmingly positive. People want us to focus on Quality—and TARGETED TRAINING is the solution to their adult educational needs."

Manufacturing Skill Standards Council (MSSC)
Independent Assessment Report to UAW-Ford

"TARGETED TRAINING was highly effective in raising awareness and transferring knowledge about Quality. A large majority of workers training under TARGETED TRAINING are still applying knowledge learned."

"TARGETED TRAINING created a well-respected quality curriculum . . . that is comprehensive, targeted to different levels and adaptable to individual plant needs."

Juanita Quann
UAW Coordinator
Equality & Diversity

"TARGETED TRAINING is the perfect 'Just-in-Time' educational solution for Equality and Diversity issues in the workplace. Our members were enthusiastic and passionate about the curriculum when we piloted the Targeted Training materials last year. We now have a "library" of different TARGETED TRAINING modules that address various subjects, such as Discrimination, Prejudice and Bias. These modules may be accessed immediately by Supervisors and Work Group Leaders, so they can PROACTIVELY address any and all situations that occur at our facilities. It's been a pleasure to work with Dennis O'Connor and Penny Drain on this exciting project."

Edie M. Reaves
Quality, Operational Excellence & Materials Manager
Hayes Lemmerz International, Inc.
(Former Manager, Ford Motor Company)

"The Targeted Training Program provides a new benchmark and innovative approach to training in very succinct single topic lessons designed for short, real time delivery in production environments.

Mr. O'Connor exhibits fantastic facilitation skills and mediation techniques . . . he is very well organized and always on time to planned targets and milestone.

Ms. Drain exhibits a very thorough expertise in adult education and ensures that materials are simple and thorough for full comprehension across the entire workforce."

Credentials

Dennis (DOC) O'Connor

D ENNIS (DOC) O'CONNOR is the President of *DOCOM Consulting, LLC.* He has more than 24 years of experience in the training, marketing and communications industries. Dennis began his career as a journalist, serving as the Managing Sports Editor for the *Observer & Eccentric Newspapers* in suburban Detroit for 10 years.

Prior to *DOCOM*, DOC served as a Vice President-Training Operations Director for a Detroit-based agency, focusing on the successful delivery of training projects for Detroit-area clients. DOC received his Master's in Business Administration (MBA) from Wayne State University (Detroit), specializing in Management and Marketing. He earned his Bachelor's Degree and Secondary Teaching Certification from the University of Michigan-Ann Arbor, majoring in Journalism and Mathematics. DOC also is a Certified Focus Group Moderator from the Burke Institute in Cincinnati.

Selected Accomplishments:

- Developed and launched multiple training and communication initiatives for UAW-represented employees in the areas of Diversity, Quality, Health & Safety and Technical Skills.
- Designed and executed a multi-million dollar Automotive "Training Matrix" program—a comprehensive creative solution to integrating all the training, database and rewards programs for dealership personnel.
- Designed, developed and serviced a multi-million dollar, co-op incentive program for Motorola Paging. Served as an extension of Motorola's marketing staff. Traveled all over the country and made

sales presentations to the Marketing Directors of Motorola's top customers

- Organized and facilitated an extensive recruiting/hiring process for a $12-million Saturn launch-training initiative.
- Managed vision alignment and business objectives during a reorganization process for 6-person sports department in the newspaper industry.

Memberships include:

- Trustee, Novi Board of Education
- Novi Community Education Advisory Council
- Michigan Minority Business Development Council (MMBDC)
- American Marketing Association (AMA)-Detroit Chapter
- National Writers Union, UAW Local 1981/AFL-CIO
- Former Member, Newspaper Guild writers union

If you have any questions about the TARGETED TRAINING concept, you can reach O'Connor at 248-880-5000.

Penny A. Drain

Penny A. Drain has 27 years of consulting, instructional design, and facilitation experience with various industries including manufacturing, utility, health services, managed care organizations, education, government, retail, and non-profit. Penny has worked extensively in the area of safety, quality, diversity and processes within manufacturing, utilities and managed-care organizations.

She has developed "Manufacturing 101" sessions for Tier I auto suppliers. These sessions involve:

- Concern Reports
- CIP
- Control Plans
- Solving Customer Problems
- Housekeeping

- Health & Safety issues
- IPFMEA
- Reducing Scrap
- Leveled Scheduling

She also has designed and developed problem solving/quality tools sessions for Tier I auto suppliers, utilities, governments and managed care. These sessions involve:

- Brainstorming
- Forcefield Analysis
- Gap Analysis
- 5 Whys
- Cause & Effect (Fishbone)
- Process Flow Diagram
- Trend Chart
- Pareto Chart
- Histogram
- Scatter Diagram
- Multi-voting
- Decision Grids
- Plan-Do-Check-Act
- Collaborated on integrating a corporate Quality Service Process based on the Malcolm Baldrige criteria within a utility company
- Facilitated Business Process Analysis (Mapping), Problem Solving/ Decision Making and Quality Team sessions

Ms. Drain earned a Bachelor of Arts Degree from the Ohio University. She has continued her education in various instructional areas i.e., *Systematic Teamwork, Problem Solving, Problem Solving and Planning, Instructional Design and Development, Developing Procedures, Policies and Documentation, Project Management, Time Management and Facilitation Skills.*

If you have any questions about the TARGETED TRAINING concept, you can reach Drain at 248-880-5000.

APPENDIX D

Samples

SAMPLE

SAMPLE
SEXUAL HARASSMENT
TARGETED TRAINING
Single Topic Lesson

What Is Sexual Harassment?

Sexual harassment is a form of sex discrimination that violates Title VII of the Civil Rights Act of 1964. Title VII of the Civil Rights Act of 1964 forbids employers with 15 or more employees to discriminate on the basis of race, color, sex, religion or national origin.

"Unwelcome sexual advances, requests for sexual favors, and other verbal or physical contact of a sexual nature constitute sexual harassment when:

1) Submission to such conduct is made either explicitly or implicitly a term or condition of an individual's employment.

2) Submission to or rejection of such conduct by an individual is used as the basis for employment decisions affecting such individuals.

3) Such conduct has the purpose or effect of unreasonably interfering with an individual's work performance or creating an intimidating, hostile, or offensive working environment."

-- *The Equal Employment Opportunity Commission (EEOC)*

Two Types of Sexual Harassment

1 **Quid Pro Quo** occurs when submission to unwelcome sexual advances or other verbal or physical conduct of a sexual nature is a term or condition, implicitly or explicitly, of an individual.

Quid Pro Quo – *"an exchange of one thing for another"*

Example of Quid Pro Quo:
- A person with supervisory responsibilities may:
    - Promise an employee a raise if he/she goes on a date with him/her.
    - Threaten an employee that he/she will be fired if he/she does not engage in sex.

2 **Hostile Environment** occurs when unwelcome sexual advances or other verbal or physical conduct of a sexual nature unreasonably interferes with an individual's work performance or creates an intimidating, hostile or offensive working environment.

A Hostile Environment:
- Can be created by anyone in the work environment (i.e., supervisors, other employees or customers)
- For it to be a "Hostile Environment" the conduct must occur on a regular or repetitive basis

Examples of a Hostile Environment:
- Sexual materials
- Physical contact in the work environment (*i.e., stalking, physical assault, coerced sexual activity*)
- Cartoons or posters of a sexual nature
- Vulgar or lewd conduct (*leering, staring, gesturing, scantily-clad individuals*)
- Obscene comments (*jokes, commenting on appearance*)
- Touching or fondling
- Written abuse (*i.e., e-mail, letters, notes*)

<table>
<tr><td>

SAMPLE

SEXUAL HARASSMENT

TARGETED TRAINING

Facilitator Guide

</td><td>

</td></tr>
</table>

Before the Lesson:

1. Review the Single Topic Lesson (STL).
2. Review this Facilitator Guide.
3. Understand that the purpose of this STL is to understand the basic concepts of Sexual Harassment (*i.e., the definition, types of sexual harassment, and examples of sexual harassment*).
4. Use examples of any cases of Sexual Harassment in your plant or facility to help illustrate the concepts in this lesson.
5. Choose the most appropriate video clips to use during this module.

BEST—Presentation Tips:

Incorporate the following bullet points as cornerstones of good presentations:

- **B**e Prepared!
- **E**nthusiastic delivery, **E**mphasize key points, **E**ncourage questions
- **S**peak clearly, loudly, and confidently
- **T**ell participants what you're going to tell them (state purpose), then tell them (deliver lesson), then tell them what you told them (summarize).

During the Lesson:

1. Introduce the STL by reviewing with participants the purpose stated in the *Before the Lesson* section—why participants need to know this and what participants need to do with it.
2. Distribute the Pre-Test tool and allow participants time to complete (approximately 5 minutes).
3. Explain that the purpose of the test is to determine participants' knowledge of the lesson.
4. Collect the Pre-Test tool and then distribute the STL and allow a few minutes for participants to read. As participants read the STL, review the Pre-Test and make sure you emphasize points that the participants missed.
5. Review the information in the left-hand column by stressing the following points:

   - Sexual harassment is a form of sexual discrimination
   - Sexual harassment violates the Civil Rights Act (*which is a law*)
   - When a person says "stop", "no," etc. it means that the advances, requests or contact is unwelcome. Any unwelcome behavior stops at this point.
   - Explicitly means: fully revealed or expressed without vagueness, implication, or ambiguity—leaving no question as to meaning or intent (explicit instructions)
   - Implicitly means: without doubting or questioning
   - Points 1 and 2 are Quid Pro Quo and Point 3 is Hostile Environment

6. Use video clips to generate discussion of Sexual Harassment (*quid pro quo and hostile work environment*).

Ask Discussion Questions:

- Use the video clips to determine:

   - Is the behavior sexual harassment?
   - If yes, what type of sexual harassment is it?
   - If no, is the behavior still inappropriate for work?

Summary and Test:

- Restate the purpose of the Single Topic Lesson to summarize.
- Distribute the Post-Test to each participant and give them 5 minutes to complete **INDIVIDUALLY.**
- After completing the Post-Test, review **AS A GROUP** to insure transfer of learning.

DENNIS O'CONNOR/PENNY DRAIN

<table>
<tr><td>

SAMPLE

SEXUAL HARASSMENT

TARGETED TRAINING

TEST

</td><td></td></tr>
</table>

1. Sexual harassment is a form of _____ discrimination.
2. Sexual harassment violates Title VII of the _____ _____ _____ of 1964.
3. What type of sexual advances, requests for sexual favors and other verbal or physical contact of a sexual nature constitute sexual harassment?

   a. Welcome
   b. Unwelcome
   c. Wanted
   d. a and c

4. Name two types of sexual harassment.

   a. _____
   b. _____

5. _____ _____ _____ occurs when submission to unwelcome sexual advances or other verbal or physical conduct of a sexual nature is a term or condition, implicitly or explicitly, of an individual.

6. _____ _____ occurs when unwelcome sexual advances or other verbal or physical conduct of a sexual nature unreasonably interferes with an individual's work performance or creates an intimidating, hostile or offensive working environment.

7. A hostile environment can be created by anyone in the work environment (i.e., *supervisors, other employees or customers*)

   a. True   b. False

8. The following are examples of _____ _____ _____:
• A person with supervisory responsibilities may:

   • Promise an employee a raise if he/she goes on a date with him/her
   • Threaten an employee that he/she will be fired if he/she does not engage in sex

9. The following are examples of _____ _____:

• Sexual materials
• Physical contact in the work environment (*i.e., stalking, physical assault, coerced sexual activity*)
• Cartoons or posters of a sexual nature
• Vulgar or lewd conduct (*leering, staring, gesturing, scantily-clad individuals*)
• Obscene comments (*jokes, commenting on appearance*)
• Touching or fondling
• Written abuse (*i.e., e-mail, letters, notes*)

	SAMPLE	
	ENERGY CONTROL AND POWER LOCKOUT	
	Observation Checklist	

Observer Directions:

- Use this tool to document your observation of partial compliance (PC) or non-compliance (NC) to ECPL procedures.
- Check the appropriate level of compliance and provide additional detail in the Operation/Explanation column.

Rating: *(PC) partial compliance*   *(NC) non-compliance*

Employee	Date	PC	NC	Operation/Explanation

TARGETED TRAINING PROGRAM

SAMPLE CURRICULUM PATH

What?— These are basic, foundational, knowledge-based modules, focused on Diversity. These Targeted Training modules are for individuals who are new to Your Company, or who need a refresher or reinforcement of your existing Diversity training programs. New employees should learn these modules AFTER receiving the Diversity Training Orientation Program. These "WHAT" modules should be reviewed and taken BEFORE the "HOW" modules.

How?— These modules are the skill and application-based modules. These modules are for individuals who are not demonstrating and/or applying the lessons learned in the "WHAT" knowledge-based modules.

Why?— These modules answer the question *"Why is Diversity considered a priority for Your Company?"* These modules are for individuals who do not understand or demonstrate the importance of Diversity at Your Company.

#	WHAT?
1	What is Diversity?
2	Common Characteristics of Diversity
3	Introducing Ourselves to Workplace Diversity
4	Recognize Prejudices/Biases/Stereotypes
5	Behaviors Related to Prejudices/Biases/Stereotypes
6	Prejudices: Impact on Performance and Productivity
7	The Importance of Perception/Assumptions/Impressions
8	Organizational Environments
9	EEO and Affirmative Action
10	What Is Inclusion?

11	Behavior Awareness Model

#	HOW?
12	Behaviors for Working Effectively With Each Other
13	Biases: Impact on Personal/Work Group Performance
14	Group Dynamics
15	Communication Skills
16	Communication Gaps
17	Inclusion Tools
18	Diversity "Change Agent" Skills
19	Leveling and Diversity "Change-Agent" Behavior
20	Business Awareness Model: Impact on Behavior
21	Diversity Action Plans

#	WHY?
22	The Business Case for Diversity: Population Environmental Trends
23	The Business Case for Diversity: Impact on Business (Buying Power)
24	The Business Case for Diversity: Diversity & Everyday

#	GEOGRAPHIC/OPERATING UNIT TOPICS
25	Recognizing Geographic/Operating Unit Biases
26	Geographic/Operating Unit Biases: Impact on Performance
27	Strategies for Emergency Situations: Dealing with Differences
28	Strategies for Emergency Situations: Prevent or Reduce Conflict
29	Strategies for Emergency Situations: Respectful Communication

#	SUPPLEMENTAL MODULES
1	Action Plans and Checklists
2	True Meaning of Inclusion (*6 Different Video Vignettes*)
3	Prejudices Supplemental (*Class Divided Video*)
4	First Impressions (*Lunch Date Video*)

HEALTH & SAFETY
INDIVIDUAL ROLES & RESPONSIBILITIES
Module 1—On-the-Job Application
Guide to Conducting Conversations

DOCUMENT: HS-RR-1 **APPROVED: August, 2008**

SAMPLE

Positioning Statement

This document is intended to prepare you for a one-on-one conversation with an employee, in accordance with health & safety guidelines.

The conversation should focus on each employee's ACTUAL job and ACTUAL responsibilities, as they relate to supporting our health & safety system.

What Is This Template Used For?

A one-on-one (1-1) conversation to determine a Skilled Tradesperson's awareness of:

☐ The plant's Health & Safety Systems
☐ His/Her role, responsibilities and rights relative to the Health & Safety and your contract
☐ How these roles are supported everyday in order to relentlessly focus on Health & Safety

What Is In This Package?

1) Guide to conducting conversations about Roles & Responsibilities
2) Safety Requirement Checklist
3) Skilled Tradesperson Conversation Guide Action Plan Guide
4) Action Plan and Tracking Tool

Who Uses This Package?

☐ Supervisor and/or Manufacturing Advisors
☐ Work Group Leaders
☐ Safety Engineers & Safety Representatives
☐ Others

One-On-One Conversation

<u>DO</u>

1. Explain the objective (*familiarity with the plant's health &safety system*)
   * Emphasize a relentless daily focus on Health & Safety, and to ensure people have the necessary skills and tools to do their jobs
   * Further emphasize that this conversation is <u>not</u> a one-stop session because of our relentless daily focus on Health & Safety
   * Be respectful:
      * Acknowledge the Skilled Tradespersons' experiences with Safety Requirements
2. Encourage Skilled Tradespersons to ask questions and respond to issues as they arise
3. Note any Health & Safety and/or training discrepancies, deficiencies, and omissions, identify action steps and then tell Skilled Tradespersons when you will get back with them
4. Conclude conversation

<u>DON'T</u>

1) Don't talk down to them
2) Don't come across as 'the expert'

Follow-up

1. Prepare action plan to address Health & Safety and training issues identified in the conversation, if any
2. Initiate follow-up conversation with Skilled Tradespersons to respond to issues identified in the conversation

| DOCUMENT: HS-RR-1 | APPROVED: August, 2008 |

How Should You Prepare For the 1-1 Conversation?

1. Complete the Health & Safety Roles & Responsibilities Targeted Training modules.
2. Review appropriate JSAs.
3. Read and understand the Skilled Tradespersons':

    a. Health & Safety requirements
    b. Roles, responsibilities and rights in your contract

4. Know location of Health & Safety materials at the workstation.
5. Review the Health & Safety Requirement Checklist.

Prepare for the Session:

Thoroughly review information supporting the following bullet topics, and the Guides included in this package, to engage the Skilled Tradesperson in a conversation on:

- His/her roles and responsibilities for Health & Safety requirements. Emphasize that this is how the Skilled Tradesperson ensures a relentless daily focus on Health & Safety
- Additional Health & Safety roles and responsibilities based on your Contract

| HEALTH & SAFETY |
| INDIVIDUAL ROLES & RESPONSIBILITIES |
| *Module 1—On-the-Job Application* |
| **Guide to Conducting Conversations** |

DOCUMENT: HS-RR-1　　　　　　　　　　**APPROVED: August, 2008**

Conduct the Session:

1. Set the stage for the conversation with the Skilled Tradesperson:

   - State the purpose of the conversation
   - Show respect for and view the Skilled Tradesperson as "the expert"
   - Link to Health & Safety Principles
   - State how this impacts the Skilled Tradesperson

2. During the conversation, discuss the following:

   - The employee's role and responsibility for Health & Safety requirements
   - Health & Safety elements at that employee's workstation regarding:

     1. Work Rules
     2. Pre-Task Analysis
     3. PPE Requirements
     4. Walking Warning Surface
     5. PMHV
     6. ECPL

   - Additional Health & Safety roles and responsibilities based on your Contract

3. Review the Health & Safety Requirement Checklist and Skilled Tradesperson Conversation Guide
4. Provide the Skilled Tradesperson Conversation Guide to the employee in advance. Fill-out the blanks at the top prior to handing out the document. Be sure to ask "open-ended" questions to promote a good discussion.
5. Emphasize the importance of the follow-up activities

Use Action Plan Tool (as appropriate):

1. Review the information in the left-hand column of the Action Plan Guide for support. Stress the following topics:

   - Who completes and uses the Action Plan/Tracking Tool
   - What to do with the Action/Plan/Tracking Tool
   - Why an Action Plan/Tracking Tool should be used

2. Explain the grid in the right-hand column:

   a. Is divided by training and Health & Safety actions
   b. States actions that you may need to take as a result of the 1-on-1 conversation
   c. Identifies resources

3. Emphasize the importance communicating actions taken as a follow-up activity with the Skilled Tradesperson

HEALTH & SAFETY

INDIVIDUAL ROLES & RESPONSIBILITIES

Module 1—On-the-Job Application

Health & Safety Requirement Checklist

DOCUMENT: HS-RR-1   **APPROVED: August, 2008**

The following form is used by the *Supervisor and/or Work Group Leader* as a "checklist" to ensure all appropriate items are reviewed during the conversation:

Skilled Tradesperson's Name: _____

Work Station: _____

Supervisor and/or Work Group Leader: _____

Which of the following did you review, demonstrate and explain to the Skilled Tradesperson on his/her job?

- { } Work Rules (e.g. work orders)
- { } Pre-Task Analysis (e.g. review available JSA)
- { } PPE Requirements (e.g. safety glasses, ear plugs, etc.)
- { } Interaction with Production Group (e.g. Access to equipment)
- { } Walking Warning Surface (e.g. international symbols and signs)
- { } PMHV (e.g. lifting and replacement of heavy equipment)
- { } ECPL (e.g. procedures for control of all energy sources)

During your conversation, did you show the Skilled Tradesperson how to *access* each of the following?

{ } Yes { }	No Work Order
{ } Yes { }	No JSA
{ } Yes { }	No PPE Requirements and Accessibility
{ } Yes { }	No Proper Contacts with Production Group
{ } Yes { }	No Safe Work Rules (e.g. confined space entry, hot work permits)
{ } Yes { }	No PMHV (e.g. who to contact, unit lockout / tag out procedures)

If there are any elements identified above that were not appropriately reviewed, (*or require follow-up and further training*), please include them in the action plan.

(See 'Action Plan Guide')

HEALTH & SAFETY
INDIVIDUAL ROLES & RESPONSIBILITIES
Module 1—On-the-Job Application
Health & Safety Requirement Checklist

DOCUMENT: HS-RR-1	APPROVED: August, 2008

OPTIONAL

The following may be used by the *Skilled Tradesperson* to prepare for the 1-on-1 session:

Skilled Tradesperson's Name: _____

Work Station: _____

Supervisor and/or Work Group Leader: _____

1. **Do you know how to *access* the following? If you do not know, then be sure your Supervisor and/or Work Group Leader shows you during the review.**

   { } Yes { }   No Work Order
   { } Yes { }   No JSA
   { } Yes { }   No PPE Requirements and Accessibility
   { } Yes { }   No Proper Contacts with Production Group
   { } Yes { }   No Safe Work Rules
                   (e.g. confined space entry, hot work permits)
   { } Yes { }   No PMHV (e.g. who to contact, unit lockout / tag out procedures)

2. Be prepared to review the following with your Supervisor and/or Work Group Leader during the 1-on-1 review. Be sure to address any issues or questions to your Supervisor and/or Work Group Leader during the review.

   { } Work Rules (e.g. work orders)
   { } Pre-Task Analysis (e.g. review available JSA)
   { } PPE Requirements (e.g. safety glasses, ear plugs, etc.)
   { } Interaction with Production Group (e.g. Access to equipment)
   { } Walking Warning Surface (e.g. international symbols and signs)
   { } PMHV (e.g. lifting and replacement of heavy equipment)
   { } ECPL (e.g. procedures for control of all energy sources)

Who

Supervisor, Work Group Leader and/or Safety Engineer

What

Health & Safety and training issues may arise during the discussion with the Skilled Tradesperson that cannot be resolved during the initial conversation. Develop an action plan that includes how the issues will be resolved. *(Reference and/or use the attached action-planning tool as appropriate.)*

Use the data collected from the 1-on-1 conversation:

- Recorded on the Health & Safety Requirement Checklist
- Health & Safety concerns identified by the Skilled Tradesperson
- Resource issues identified

Analyze and take action on all data collected, as appropriate.

Why

To track and take action on training and/or Health & Safety issues that were discovered during the 1-on-1 conversation.

Issue	Action	Resources
Training	ω Identify appropriate Safety expert	ω Appropriate training materials
	ω Identify and schedule Safety "Targeted Training" as necessary	ω "Targeted Training" courses
	ω Ensure Safety requirements are available and up-to-date at the workstation	ω Appropriate Health & Safety Personnel at your location
	ω Prioritize Safety training, based on overall needs of the Skilled Tradesperson	ω "Targeted Training" courses
Health & Safety	ω Identify appropriate support systems, as required	ω Employee involvement ω Visual aids, preventive maintenance ω Health & Safety audits ω Health & Safety JSAs ω Coordinators/Analysts
	ω Review your Contract, as necessary	ω "Best in Class" Health & Safety Program, Local Health & Safety Rep.
	ω Assist the Skilled Tradesperson in understanding the plant's process for raising Health & Safety concerns	ω Local Health & Safety Committee process, contract, JSAs, "Targeted Training" courses
	ω Immediately address any Health & Safety concern, implement appropriate containment measures, and restart operation	ω Contract, Local Health & Safety Committee process
	ω Enlist the assistance of the following as necessary: 1. Local Unit Health & Safety Representative 2. Local Health & Safety Committee 3. Operations/Division Health & Safety Committee 4. National Health & Safety Committee	ω Provide representative and committee functions and responsibilities
Follow-Up Conversation	ω Schedule follow-up conversation (*more than one if necessary*)	ω Provide resources required to complete conversation(s).

HEALTH & SAFETY
INDIVIDUAL ROLES & RESPONSIBILITIES
Module 1—On-the-Job Application
Action Plan Tracking Tool

DOCUMENT: HS-RR-1   APPROVED: August, 2008

ACTION PLAN AND TRACKING TOOL

Training √	Health & Safety √	Issue	Corrective Action	Responsibility	Date Due

	SAMPLE IMPLEMENTING Targeted Training SAMPLE Evaluation Tool				

Session Date and Time: _____

Name: _____
(optional)

Directions: Use the following scale to indicate your level of agreement with the statements below. If you rate at a level of 1, 2 or 3 please provide a written explanation in the "comments" section or discuss with your facilitator.

Rating: 1= strongly disagree; 2= disagree; 3= neither agree nor disagree; 4= agree; 5= strongly agree; NA= not applicable

	1	2	3	4	5	NA
Session Content:						
1. Flowed in a logical sequence.						
2. Was easy to understand.						
3. Was aligned with the session learning objectives.						
4. Was complete and up to date.						
5. Was relevant to my job.						
Single Topic Lessons and Test Materials:						
6. Were well organized.						
7. Were written in a way to help me learn.						
8. Were appropriate for this session.						
9. Will be useful after the session.						
Facilitator Guide Materials:						
10. Were well organized.						
11. Were written in a way to help me learn.						
12. Were appropriate for this session.						
13. Were visually engaging.						
14. Will be useful after the session.						
Session Facilitator(s):						
15. Were knowledgeable of the session process and topic.						
16. Provided clear directions.						
17. Encouraged discussion and questioning.						
18. Kept discussion and activities on track.						
19. Provided feedback.						
Training Approach and Activities:						
20. Were appropriate for the audience.						
21. Were appropriate for the content.						
22. Were engaging.						
23. Provided me with enough time.						
24. Facilitated my learning.						

DENNIS O'CONNOR/PENNY DRAIN

<table>
<tr><td colspan="2">SAMPLE
IMPLEMENTING
Targeted Training
SAMPLE Evaluation Tool</td><td></td></tr>
</table>

Directions: Use the following scale to indicate your level of agreement with the statements below. If you rate at a level of 1, 2 or 3 please provide a written explanation in the "comments" section or discuss with your instructor *(Train-the-Trainer and Pilots only).*

Rating: 1= strongly disagree; 2= disagree; 3= neither agree nor disagree; 4= agree; 5= strongly agree; NA= not applicable

	1	2	3	4	5	NA
Training Environment:						
25. Was appropriate for the session purpose.						
26. Was comfortable.						
27. Was free from distractions.						
28. Was easily accessible.						
29. Enabled me to learn.						
Training session impacted me by:						
30. Increasing my knowledge of this session topic.						
31. Increasing my confidence and ability to transfer my knowledge to my workplace.						
32. Making me willing to encourage others to participate.						
33. Satisfying me with the overall training.						

Additional Comments (i.e., *what I liked about the session; recommendations for improvement; comments for 1, 2, 3 levels*):

	SAMPLE
SAMPLE **IMPLEMENTING** **Targeted Training** **SAMPLE Observation Tool**	

Observed: _____

Did the Observed Facilitator:

	Behavior	Yes	No	Comments
1.	Review Single Topic Lesson (STL) purpose. How does the lesson affect your job?			
2.	Provide participants the STL and Tests?			
3.	Understand the content of the Targeted Training module?			
4.	Provide the necessary examples?			
5.	Use STL discussion questions?			
6.	Ask and answer relevant questions?			
7.	Encourage participants to engage in discussion?			
8.	Explain how he/she would support the importance lesson on the job site?			

DENNIS O'CONNOR/PENNY DRAIN

SAMPLE IMPLEMENTING **Targeted Training** SAMPLE Observation Tool	

Did the Observed Facilitator:

Behavior	Yes	No	Comments
9. Summarize by restating the STL purpose?			
10. Use the **BEST** Presentation Tips?			

Additional Comments:

TARGETED TRAINING
SAMPLE AUDIT CHECKLIST

☐	IMPLEMENTATION PROCESS & PLAN
	Reviewed all Targeted Training materials and Recommended Curriculum Path to develop a local training implementation plan.
	Reviewed the appropriate Operational Training Matrix Analysis and job classification/group listing.
	Identified what curriculum component, at which level, is required for a given employee or work group.
	Accessed the required training materials on your intranet website
	Ensured that he/she had the correct course Single Topic Lesson (STL), Facilitator Guide and Test for their Operation.
	Reviewed any supplemental materials for the course that could be useful.
	The Supervisor and Work Group Leader reviewed the Facilitator Guide for the course.
	All Top-Level Managers, Area Managers and/or Superintendents reviewed the material with the Supervisor prior to presentation to an employee or work group.
	The Area Manager and/or Superintendent ensured that the Supervisor was adequately familiar with the material and capable of delivering the Single Topic Lessons effectively.
	The Supplemental Material Single Topic Lessons on *Presentation Skills* and *How to Deliver an STL* was reviewed with Supervisors prior to delivery.
	Scheduled the session for the appropriate employee or work group.

☐	OBSERVE A TARGETED TRAINING SESSION
	Administered the pre-assessment to the appropriate employee or work group before, or in advance of, the scheduled training course.
	Delivered the selected Single Topic Lesson
	Ensured that appropriate attendance was taken at the session
	Reviewed with the participants the immediate application of the learning to their job
	Reviewed the STL's purpose, why participants needed to know this and what participants needed to do with it
	Explained the Pre-Test's purpose (*to determine participants' knowledge of the lesson*)
	Distributed the Pre-Test tool. Read each test question aloud, allowing time for the participants to answer the questions.
	Collected the Pre-Test tool and then distributed the STL and allowed a few minutes for participants to review. If feasible, reviewed the Pre-Tests as participants read the STL. During instruction, read aloud each section in the STL where the Pre-Test answers can be found. This helps to emphasize key elements missed in the pre-tests.
	Emphasized those learning topics which were identified as concerns in the Pre-Test
	Demonstrated energy and passion
	Spoke clearly and loud enough
	Moved around the room as he/she spoke
	Demonstrated good body posture and eye contact
	Spoke with confidence and authority
	Lesson was logically organized
	Talked with the participants; created rapport
	Finished on time and allowed time for questions
	Was prepared

	Summarized all Key Concepts in the STL
	Answered Questions from the Participants
	Administered the Post-Test. Gave each employee time to complete the test individually. Employees used the STL during the Post-Test • Once all employees had adequate time to complete the assessment, reviewed the test answers, as a group. Ensured that any employees with questions get clarification and coaching, as required. • Allowed the employees to keep Post-Test or reference, along with their copy of the appropriate Single Topic Lesson.

☐	**TRACKING, REPORTING, ETC.**
	Any employee requiring additional coaching, after the Post-Test, received further STL content review until the knowledge was transferred.
	All training records are maintained by the responsible persons in your organization
	All Targeted Training Modules were delivered by the employees' Supervisor and/or Work Group Leader. Note: Supervisors responsible for multiple work groups should rotate around to each group. If there is no Work Group Leader, the Supervisor should do the training.
	Updated the employees training record, per the facility's Training Tracking Procedure. Note: All employee training records should travel with the employee should they change jobs or facilities.
☐	**TRANSFER OF LEARNING**
	Employees acted on the information provided during the STL. What did they do?
	Used the Post-Test and/or Observation Tools to reinforce the transfer of learning. How did they reinforce the transfer of learning?
	How has Targeted Training impacted your business unit? Any measurable results?

Re-examine Your Training Resources

DECIDING TO TURN your company's training program upside down is not an easy decision to make. You have probably invested thousands (*if not millions*) of dollars over the years developing classroom training or computer-based courseware. Repurposing those materials into 30-minute chunks might seem like pointless rework.

But nothing could be further from the truth.

The truth is that most training interventions you conduct, according to the old model, are essentially throwing good money after bad. Why should you continue spending money for instructors, binder printing, web design and courseware updates when the results will continue to be disappointing? Besides, who has the TIME to schedule full-day seminars for all workers?

How can you know for sure that you are currently wasting resources? Take a moment and think back to your own training:

- How many key facts can you remember from training classes?
- Can you remember which class was responsible for which fact?
- Can you remember the context in which the fact was presented?
- Did you ever apply that knowledge to your work?

Now, think about the information you use every day in your workplace. If you are like most people, you can remember the person that gave you the information, and the context in which they offered it to you.

We can all remember the boss that helped us learn the right way to do a task, or the co-worker that show us a Best Practice.

TARGETED TRAINING plays to the *strength and power* of working relationships, and it is formatted in a way that ensures a strong, "learn-do" connection.

It's hard to argue against the fact the TARGETED TRAINING is a revolutionary approach—30 minutes of focused training content administered on a monthly or weekly basis, year after year; instead of a three-day "data dump" once every year or two.

Even if you take a "toe-in-the-water" approach to adopting TARGETED TRAINING, you will have better results than avoiding the inevitable. Short-cycle, high-frequency training will be the way knowledge is acquired in the years that lay ahead.

So why not get started this year?

And, if you and your company are passionate about becoming a learning organization, you must consider a full-scale adoption of the TARGETED TRAINING approach.

You really can't afford not to . . .